Angelic Messenger

A Man's Quest to Become an Angel of God

SHAWN LANGE

Runner up in the New England Book Festival
Honorable mention New York Book Festival
Honorable mention Los Angeles Book Festival
Boca Ceiga High School Pirates Gulfport, Florida

IMPORTANT PAGE WRITE REVIEW!

Post a review on my website, thanks.
Website: www.ShawnLange.com
To e-mail the author: ShawnLange36@yahoo.com

Special thanks to my contributors:
My children who sacrificed the most, to my children
and grand and great grandchildren,
My mothers, fathers, my brothers, Aunt Cindy
Rick and Mary Joyner
Jim and Alexandra Kingzett Papa and Mamma Callicoat
Mr. and Mrs. George E. Tragos Esq.
Cynthia Wurner (editor) and Jennifer Webb
Martin Luther King Jr. Mr. and Mrs. O'Dell Owen (Cedartown, Ga.)

PREFACE

I am on a quest from the missions of God that sent me from the glory of communion, filling me with the blood of Christ, with God-like speed that sails me down the Universe. From out of my bellows, I pray to God as He journeys to my presence, He is not far from me now!

God's blessings upon you my Angels with mercy that pleases my thoughts, by the scent of your senses for your mass have been long overdue. In the glory of your presence in my eyes that will make me that soul in you again my beloved brothers & confidants, we will be together soon.

Cataclysmic results of good superseding all evil! Trajectory triangulated annihilating any threatening incoming presence either spiritually or telepathically, this binds Angels with your presence.

My absolute desire to become an Angel of God was just a shimmer of light, the fervor of the Lord's excitement, knowing what kind of exuberance we would receive when we deliver our messages.

I amass the secrets about life after death, the stories about the deception of Adam and Eve, and how the battle of principalities was won. I explain how Satan foraged his own Empire to fight against our Republic, our Heavenly Father, and Christ in Heaven.

CONTENTS

Part 1
Autobiography

INTRODUCTION

M y journey begins in Jungle Prada, a historic location where the Spanish explorer Pánfilo de Narváez landed his monstrous ships in Florida. The day was April 15, 1528. Narváez and his five ships with a crew of three hundred men landed where Saint Petersburg is now. This five-ship armada was the first landing on the peninsula known as Florida, in a jungle called Prada. Back then, the area was a natural rain forest. It was the location for the first Easter celebration in North America.

Narváez expected to see lions, tigers, and elephants, but the only thing he found was the riches of a lush Florida landscape, wonderful climate, and a tribe of curious Indians. The story takes place in Jungle Prada where my family lived. It was not an easy life even though this jungle calmed my spirit with its vibrant thick green foliage.

My life started with an abusive father torturing my mother while being involved in drugs. Father tormented mother to the point that it caused wickedness to permeate throughout the house. I was plagued with an ominous presence that coveted my demise. This evil presence took me through physical, mental, and spiritual crises—even catastrophe—many times. Yet I am alive because of God's grace and protection. I know that my past journey has become today's mission, not only to atone for my own sins, but also to tell my story so that others will benefit.

With Jungle Prada being a backdrop, I tell a story of how I came to witness, visually and audibly, the supernatural. I have repented, atoned, and sought salvation every moment of every day. My opposition starts out with my father, but the real antagonist was Satan. Then I was taken into darkness, deceived by a priest who led me into a pit of despair that would lead ultimately to madness. Even I turned against my own best wishes after many poor decisions that left me vulnerable to a priest who was a conjurer of darkness.

I married at sixteen, fathered three children, and started and ran a successful business. Seen as a kind of working-class hero, I went astray—largely because of drugs, as you will see— and lost everything, including my own life. This story almost ends with my drowning in the Gulf of Mexico, surrounded by hammerhead sharks. The circumstances of my survival and rescue are nothing less than miraculous.

A big part of my story includes messages and visions from supernatural beings that started when I was a young boy. In part two of this book, I will reveal the amazing messages given to me from the Archangel Derdekea, among others.

I have revolutionary theories about my patent that involves subatomic mass, cold fusion, and hydroelectric power. Basically, my patent is a device that purifies water while producing electricity. This machine will show how humanity must evolve to avoid utter destruction. It also can send chilled distilled water on top of a glacier to reverse global warming.

Nevertheless, reader, first, I want to tell you my own story.

CHAPTER 1

Labor Pains

June 29, 1979: Jungle Prada

My pregnant mother slips out of bed, anticipating the dawning of another Sunday morning. As our sun peers light throughout our canvas, the star begins to rise over a canopy of thick acorn trees that shades the forest's floor.

Mother's feet are swollen and on the brink of delivery, nonetheless barefooted she shuffles her way into the kitchen to make father's breakfast before he awakes. Mother waits patiently for my father to rise before serving him his breakfast. My father wakes again on the wrong side of the bed. The morning of my birth starts with pills, booze, and "Why the hell are my eggs runny?"

My mother could not complete a task without forfeiting her rights as a woman, much less an equal human being. My father was an ignorant alpha male who never understood the actual enlightenment and peace that a real father could bring. Mother knew that something was not right with me.

The fight that morning was caused by the eggs, runny like the snot down Mother's nose. She was being tortured and beaten, but it was not until the coat hanger came out that mother knew she was going to feel every blow.

Mother must have tried to shield her unborn fetus from the vicious attack that the man was delivering upon us. I must have been the bastard son of whomever, blessing our home filled with fear. With a good swift kick, poor mother must have misunderstood how much love one-man boots could hold. Finally, he kicked her hard enough, and her water broke, metaphysically speaking not in actuality.

I was on the way—an unplanned mystery, a question filled with fear and shame. My father rushed us to the hospital, blowing through every red light in a panic. Still, this man had not yet comprehended the full extent of damage that he had inflicted on Mother.

Before my eyes opened to this world, before the stitches were placed on Mother to sew up the wound from the beatings nine months earlier, God's spirit passed through to heal our house of terrors. My Lord, my Savior, my everlasting brother, stopping in to visit this unnamed fetus, not yet made aware of the numerous titles promised to me since my conception.

Ensuring that the Lord blessed my eyes, He then entered the womb of my mother to take her pain. Grandmother Clara our Native American Iroquoian, Princess dropped to her knees, asked for forgiveness for my Father Barry's actions and for Christ to remain close to her youngest grandson.

The benevolent communing of souls together is through the Only One's act of sacrifice: The Lord Jesus Christ's crucifixion and resurrection. I was an infant compared to this giant presence lying beside me in my mother's womb. The Lord Jesus Christ prepared for my delivery in the backseat of my father's Chevy. Mother was ready to give birth to any son willing to live in squalor.

As my Heavenly Father delivered us, I felt as if a part of me was missing; entering this world, I was afraid. It was as if I could see my birth through the sight of the Holy Spirit. Left without video recordings at that time, our existence was only captured through the presence of God.

We lived a modest life but didn't have a video recorder in the budget that year. Mother was bearing down and screaming in pain, and there was no sophisticated medical help to ease the terrifying pains of labor. There was something in the air, though, as if time remained motionless, while God assisted in my delivery.

Christ Jesus laid His hands upon my laboring mother to calm her fears. He gave me names, rank, and titles in His Army that day, for what I would see in the future was the birth of the antichrist, a hobbler with evil intent.

From the beginning, before I was even born at 6:26 a.m. (EST), Satan knew my name. In the years after my birth, he was watching over me, looking for a window of opportunity to strike me dead, to eliminate the threat I posed to his cause. Through the course of my life, God honored His agreement with me and my family. Even through all the hell brought upon us, if we never lost faith in Him, He would bless us eternally.

Little did I know that Satan was trying to end my life as soon as he could, since my birth meant the beginning of an end? All throughout my existence, every chance he got, he has tried literally to end my life. Left with only one defense however, God's blessing granted me the gift of sight to see past the living, into the realm of the dead. I witnessed the battle between light and dark angels.

Later, I would witness many dark things that happen to people outside their line of sight. A legion of Angels accompanied me on my journey. I could see the penumbra of their shadows, images that obscured me, like an eclipse where the light begins to bend. Marking me with their affections, for my future was blanketed with many obstacles, and it was far too dangerous for me to walk throughout life alone.

"He God has put his angels in charge of you to watch over you wherever you go." (Psalms 91:11 Max Lucado NCV)

My mother lay on that hospital bed, Father ran frantically to find a doctor to deliver me before I landed on my head. The doctor approached my mother. She pressed gently against my mother's belly to give this laboring woman the instincts to push her son's head out.

I started my descent into this world, I came ripping and tearing mother's heart apart as well. It was like lightning striking, and out came my head. There I was—a coned head with white hair, a premature infant with crystal blue eyes.

The cabinet of souls was lacking spirits willing to commit themselves to spiritual rebirth, and I was the one they wanted damned. However, those nightmares did not come until far later in life. My dad stayed within the confines of the role of a regretful father. This husband was excited to see that mother had conceived a little baby boy.

The next nine months I filled the room with new smells, like yells reigning down from above, dad shouting, Mom shaking, my brother, Alan, pissing his pants, me screaming because mother shuddered when giving me her breasts.

Now I know that my father never knew his own father, never knew if his father loved him as much as he loved Dick. Yelling and beatings were his way to get emotional release, then he put on his best threads to win mother back yet again.

Mother was getting tired of the vicious cycle of violence, conversations filled with profanity, with mountains of mortifying shame. The beatings only lessened in the last year, yet they were harder than they had ever been before.

The immense burden of this secret and having a new infant was more than this seaman could bear, and that cross was too ponderous for Mother to lift herself.

It was not long after my birth that Mother worked up the courage to leave my father for good. She was required to work two jobs. Left alone, my brother Alan and I were for the most part neglected. We had nowhere to turn to other than our beloved grandmother, Clara. She was the mortar binding the stones that built the house we lived in. With her, we found peace, safety, and refuge. Without her, our house in Jungle Prada would fall, long before it did.

CHAPTER 2

The Dome

My father was angry as usual. He had been on a six-day drug binge. Marijuana was his primary escape; however, this day Father was snorting cocaine and drinking his daily amount of alcohol. Mother was out shopping while Father attempted to babysit Alan and me. Father was preoccupied while lifting weights in the Florida room.

It was the day before my first birthday. Everyone was preparing for the barbeque to celebrate the day of my birth. Mother entered the house with her arms full of groceries. She asked my father, "Barry, if you are not too busy, could you get the rest of the groceries from the car?"

He refused to move as he stared at his muscles in front of the mirror. He was stubborn and lazy, yelling curses at Mother as if she were a dog. He sat there calling Mother Names, refusing to bow to her desires.

Dad should have witnessed the fear she had in her eyes when his temper was aroused. I was walking around the corner, afraid that with her next step, she would incur his wrath. However, it was his prerogative, and he chose to care about himself over the care and comfort of others.

My father sat there on that weight bench—yelling, digesting his booze, smoking his marijuana, and snorting his cocaine, while playing his music too loud. I stumbled my way to the edge of the newly finished living room in this lavish spread—our five bedrooms and three and a half bath domiciles with a screened-in pool.

My father was lifting weights in the Florida room. It was a day my father made an event of cutting his muscles and enjoying his drugs. Father knew nothing about how to treat a woman; his anger always kept him from loving a woman in the proper manner with loyalty and devotion.

Father was controlled by his addictions and the demon inside his heart kept coming up with more reasons to seek sexual comfort elsewhere. This was one of the many reasons that kept him from becoming a kind and loving husband or a good father.

His eyes glazed over due to the fistful of Quaaludes tablets that he had taken, having swallowed those little pills to trick his mind that he was a God.

With a genuine heart filled with humor and his love of music, his interaction with others made him the life of a party. The house smelled like Christmas in July; the smell of marijuana blown throughout the house. When I inhaled that drug at such an early age, it sure made me silly.

The smell of wild turkey on his lips smelled as pungent as a homeless person out in the cold on Christmas Eve. However, it was at the end of June, and his hot temper started a small fire as mother was preparing the bird we were about to eat. Mother's complaints got father off his workout bench to knock her around a bit. I guess her arguments were too close to dinnertime. My father's fever of anger became an inferno. He intended to smack some sense into his wife referred to as "that bitch."

He was tired of mother slamming the refrigerator door too harshly after his refusal to get up and help unload the groceries. He decided to take that beautiful woman down a peg or two. Mother was yelling, my father drew back his fist and hit her in the face.

Alan grabbed for Father's arm, biting him hard enough to leave dental impressions. A backhand across Alan's face threw his little frame across the room, landing him against the wall. Alan became a bloodcurdling frenzy. Arms and legs were flailing before he curled himself in a ball on the floor.

I was a young boy as I walked myself into the line of fire. Mother tried her best to protect me from becoming my father's next victim.

My father lacked restraint and could not curb his thirst for violence. What was in Father's heart was anger, it happened to be the strongest muscle in his body, always crushing mother's great expectations of love.

I was toddling my way toward the carport. Alan crying on the kitchen floor was something I did not wish to see. I was a baby, what could I do? I saw my father's anger as something stronger than a hurricane. When our father turned violent, he personified Darth Vader to me.

Once the argument and the whimpers of Alan's crying were over, Mother's nose rubbed raw from using her sleeve to wipe the snot and tears from her face. I could not help but be confused. All I wanted was for my father to love Mother as much as he loved his weeds. Sadness permeated the house during that terrible time.

Returning to his workout, Father started to lift those heavy objects high in the air, bench-pressing his large arms like torpedoes; they sure looked like mountains to me.

I peered around the corner, searching for something to play with, trying to leave the devastation behind in the kitchen. I was curious and unused to walking, hardly noticed by my father. I toddled over to where my father was lifting those heavy weights.

Now when my father was angry, he could only focus on one thing at a time. As it was, fate was not entirely on my side. As my father lifted those weights high in the air, I stood up to play with some of his curly black hair. That is when a one-hundred-and-eighty-pound hammer dropped straight down on my head, cracking my dome, crushing my skull in that instant. Not one drop of blood fell, only a single tear landed on the floor rendering me unconscious.

When I came to, I was screaming in pain, all my father could do was to place his hand upon my mouth. Father and Mother carried me into the bathroom to see better with the bright vanity lights. Mother looked at my crushed head. Soft and pliable, the bone that protected my brain was now crushed.

Leaning across the sink, body against the wall, Mother returned from the kitchen with a bag of frozen peas to cool down the top of my head, to keep my brain from swelling. Mother cried out at Father, "What in the hell did you do this for? You have no self-control!"

His anger was only seconds from becoming a bloody rage. The veins now extruding from his forehead, he grabbed her by the hair as she screamed for her mother. Her eyes were red from broken vessels, the salt of her tears mixed with the blood in her mouth. Repentance was her only recourse, so she pleaded with my father, "Please don't hurt me!"

My father's angry outburst filled with regret. In his grief was great sadness. He did not mean to hurt me; it was the product of his own emptiness. Breathless and hyperventilating, mother wipes the blood from her nose and mouth.

My mother's heart was made of glass—millions of fissures and cracks breaking her down, shattering her hope and longing for love.

With Father's stomach filled with a handful of Quaaludes, having no control over his environment, he went into rage again. He grabbed a towel off the shower rod, wrapped it around his fist, he began to beat mother again. Mother cowering in the bathtub, as father proceeded to strike her again and again. Mother pleaded for him to cease her punishment, hoping he would regain some level of sanity.

The sacrifice my mother endured, the physical torment, the mental agony…It was the straw that broke my father's back. I think now that his contribution was only for his own selfish agenda. I am a product of that disaster.

The screaming continued as Mother got out of the tub, she grabbed me from the bathroom sink. Taking what clothes, she could, throwing formula and diapers into her laundry basket. She unhooked her keys from the "Welcome to Our Home" plaque on the wall.

Ice melting on my head, a smile on my face, for I must have been dreaming. Slumbering without a sound; I was now unconscious. She had finally decided to leave my father for good.

She ran outside with what she had, returning for her suitcases, praying for my father to be oblivious to the back door opening and closing. The sounds of me regaining consciousness penetrated the air as I began to sob from the pain. Alan held the bag of frozen peas on my head. I needed a doctor and a hospital. Mother had made up her mind.

She had loaded the Impala with her favorite clothes— even though they were only hand-sewn rags from the secondhand store. The only people left to get hold of were her children. It made more sense than ever for Mother to escape with the young ones a couple of blocks away to Grandmother Clara's house while we were all still breathing.

There was something about waking in the morning to Mother's kisses. The smell of Grandmother Clara's fragrance in the air like fresh jasmine, with a splash of orange blossom tucked between the sheets.

Mixed with deep sorrow, the innocence of this morning due to the reality of his actions left Mother with no recourse. It was time for Dad to go! Left pondering if anyone could protect our weak and fragile home. It was time for us to find out what God had in store for us next. The tyrannical lord of the manor was replaced with something far worse.

Meanwhile, the head wound was what the doctors credited for my mental disorder, i.e., the ability to see what many were never aware of, beginning with Angels, then spirits. Despite knowing if God is real or if He cared about what happened to me.

After our father left, I guess Alan felt that he had to fight for the love and affection of our mother. As if her love was nutrients with only so much to go around. He took her focus away from me; I became the 'runt' of the litter.

As a youngster, I was happy to have a big brother even if I had to fight for my mother's attention. Having an older brother brought a sense of security to the house. In my mind, though, I was isolated. I felt as if my heart contained a single lonesome dove.

I was only a couple of years old when, after our father left, a part of me died too. It was plain to see that the lights in our eyes faded the day Dad ran away. Alan was ready to take control as the head of my father's table. He too became a father figure to me. Strong-willed, a growing young man, but with adolescent fears, angry and loveless after the loss of our father.

It was almost a year later, and my father finally allowed Alan and me to come over for the weekend. Since the house in Jungle Prada belonged to my maternal grandparents, Father was left with no place else to live.

My father's new home was a pop-up trailer in the middle of a Sarasota swamp on the outskirts of a trailer park. Father was performing some light duties at the church house. The day was joyful. We were excited to have a sleepover at my father's new place. It was not much, yet father made us feel at home. It had been many moons. I had started to believe that Father had abandoned us.

My father spent that weekend working in the trailer park. It was the day my Guardian Angel was present before me. I was to be the victim of a horrific event. An omen was about to happen. Father was repairing the church house to cover his rent. When the accident occurred, he had the two front doors of the church off the frame, placed on four sawhorses as the stain began to dry.

We were running around the front yard as Lady, our most trusted and beloved dog was chasing Alan around the playground. The mud was thick with dew that memorable morning. We were somewhere near Anna Maria Island. Lady was excited to see us again; it had been several months since we had seen her or our father.

The morning had a feeling of predictability, our dog, Lady, chasing Alan, Dad starting his chores in a new place, distant from our mother. Distracted…sensing his eyes were fixed in the wrong position from the amount of weed he had been smoking…too dangerous to have us running around the courtyard with hazards in clear view…Then it happened.

My spirit left my body the moment Lady hit me from behind, launching me headfirst toward the door, sending a rusty old door hinge plunging into my eye. As my head struck the door, the door hinge became stuck in my eye. I was gasping for breath and hyperventilating. The pain was crippling. Dad frantically rushed over, pulling the rusty hinge from my blue eye, the pride and joy of my mother.

Blood came spewing profusely from the orb of my eye. The blue-gray mist that filled the air that morning was now like blood raining down from Heaven. Puddles of blood collected on the plastic underneath my feet; the screams cut the air with the horror that the hinge pierced my eye.

The race to the hospital was a windy ride; God's Angels were with us as they were doing all they could to keep up with my father's lead foot dislodged to within the throat of that carburetor. I sat, blood-drenched towel in hand, praying for God's will to take over my body before I started to slip into that crevice. I was unable to relieve myself of the excruciating pain. I was afraid the sight of Satan's presence had blinded my eyes forever.

Arriving at the hospital, the doctors asked my family to vacate the room so the surgeons could repair my eye. They attempted to contact my mother, yet she was unavailable. Grandmother Clara got into her vintage 1967 Shelby GT Mustang, driving as fast as she could over the Skyway Bridge.

My grandmother was like the calm before a storm, her spirit overwhelmed with concern for me; her love was immeasurable, her speedometer pegged out driving her Mustang at top speeds.

At the time of the surgery, the operation must have somehow affected my eyesight, leaving me with an enhanced ability to see inside the realm of parallel universes. God gave me the gift of pure sight to see the improbable, to be able to perform unthinkable tasks. To see that God's will be my duty to act against evil by praying for those forces to be abolished. To stand against the lies and deceit, Satan's pleasure to tie to be untwisted, and unbinding lost souls attached to demons that are built upon an army of ruins.

They told my grandmother that they were going to have to operate, performing minor surgery to sew up my eye. The surgeons were ready to begin. Grandmother Clara dropped to her knees, praying that Jesus Christ and the Holy Spirit would guide the surgeon's hands to ensure a steady job. She hoped the surgeons would repair the eye without permanent or serious aftereffect to the actual sight of my eye.

I remember sitting on that table as they closed my eyes. It was as if I was having an out-of-body experience. I saw myself lying on a table, bandage wrapped around my head; my doctors surrounded that operating table, preparing my father for the worst.

It was as though I could see through the eyes of the Lord Jesus Christ as He prepared to manifest His presence by guiding the surgeon's hands throughout this procedure. Jesus was ready to overcome, by stepping inside the surgeon's body to control his hands during this delicate operation. My surgery team waited for the drugs to take effect.

After the lapse in time while waiting for the surgeons to both cleanse and clear the wound, they sewed me up. I needed several sutures altogether, causing an insufficient loss of sight. Thankfully, it was not a permanent handicap. The fact of the matter is that divine mystical forces chose me. I have always felt, even as a young boy, those great beings were watching over me.

I was called upon to witness many beautiful visions that the doctors later called schizophrenia. I knew better. This gift of supernatural sight helped the dead see the light to pass or remove themselves from their current hell into different dominions. I have conversations with the Lord Jesus Christ, delivering and receiving His messages with His Angels at my disposal. I have had many spiritual guides throughout my life that have brought many forces of energy within proximity of me.

Matriculating throughout life my most prevalent prayer was I wanted to become an Angel of God. Many have proclaimed my intelligence to be mere genius. Other evaluation of my cognitive thoughts and spiritual concepts, say my writing is brilliant. Yet, most professionals say I possess a trait, some sort of supernatural sixth senses that have led many to my presence seeking guidance.

CHAPTER 3

Color Me Purple

After my parents' marriage dissolved, our father had gone away, all that remained were the scars upon Mother's back. There were recurring nightmares, Alan and I would wake up gasping for breath, like our lungful of exhaled air had just been expelled from a tomb.

Mom and Alan developed a bond somewhat close to a maternal and paternal partnership except mother turned out to be the father figure and Alan turn out motherly, especially after Father was banished from our lives.

The winters down in Florida were always something beautiful. I think that is why most my family moved down from New York and Pennsylvania—to enjoy the palm trees and coconuts in January while the weather was mild and the beaches open.

I remember sitting on the couch watching the Macy's Day Parade with my grandmother. Grandmother Clara was holding me tightly, keeping me warm. I was turning five years old that June, I felt like I had a piece of Heaven, wrapped up in that Angel's arms.

Ever since the accident happened with my eye, it seemed that she and I were inseparable. I had a head of full of white hair, she could not resist running her fingers through it. Grandmother Clara and I sat together watching television. I loved my grandmother very much, times spent with her was always some of my favorite occasions. I think that of any one I have met on this earth; she was one of the warmest and charismatic people.

She used to call me her gangster of love. She was a special woman, a very intelligent one, medically capable of assisting in the performance of surgeries. She started to teach me to read. I was not very good at putting my thoughts to words and my words into sentences. Meanwhile, Alan was always reading over my shoulder. By the time the words made way to my mouth, Alan had already finished my sentence. Reading for me was a slow process.

My mother was going out to bars, listening to music, and dancing with our aunt Vivian. As Grandmother Clara was preparing us for bed, they were getting ready to party. I can remember telling my mother that she was beautiful with the sparkles all over her dress. Her hair was all the way down to her bottom—blonde and beautiful. With her makeup on, she looked like a supermodel. She smelled amazing. I did not want her scent to leave my senses. I wanted her to stay home and dance the night away, just the two of us.

That night, Grandmother Clara had her boyfriend over. We called him G-Jon. They had put Alan to bed. They wanted to continue teaching me more about reading out of the *Reader's Digest*. As I was struggling with it for an hour, G-Jon came up with a brilliant idea that I should read the words that stood out the most to me. As I read the words that were comprehensible, he showed me how the important words were almost brighter or bolder than the other words. As I read the passage, Jon wrote the code—the bright words—down on a tablet.

He then explained that there was a basic binary code to everything, and God's fingerprints were on all literary substance. He explained also that events happen in a cycle; therefore, the predictions are easier because they reoccur. Certain codes determine the words that stand out among other words in the literature. With these words, a hidden message forms passages that lead you to visions or dreams.

Besides the *Reader's Digest*, medical journals were also used, as well as the Holy Bible. One of the primary reasons they were teaching me to read was so that I might grow up wise and gifted—to prophetically speak and perceive the Holy Scripture as the living will of God.

After that night, I always remembered that lesson where they sat me down and taught me about how words form pictures and pictures placed on screens. Whether the words were white, or the noises were real, they all have a way of being measured and received.

I needed no machine to see or to hear white noises— it is only a pure energy source received by my brain. This gift was something I was blessed with, an inheritance of sorts that made me prophetic.

I fulfilled God's need of me becoming a soldier, able to view life after death. I had many observations behind death's shroud given to me by many celestial bodies, waiting for light to illuminate their path returning them to God's presence.

They were eager to give up their position at the frontline of chaos at the edge of death's dominion. I had visions and scenarios that brought me close to the sinister realm of sin that drives many to madness—the screams of dark angels burning innocents who had not yet had a chance to escape from hell. Those Heavenly Angels traveled often into hell to remove a spirit not deserving of fire and torture; distraught, they rescued them from Hades.

The next morning, we peered through the windowpane, seeing a mirror image of Mother's party. There were reflections of them sitting on the front patio with some existential male, tall and dainty with curly brown hair.

We confronted the images of this horse trader checking Mother out as if she were a filly in the front yard, with Grandmother Clara being better acquainted. I guess my mother was empty, needing a person in her life. She introduced us to PFC Romello Homeboy, a culinary arts soldier in the United States Army.

He was military to the core. His father was a great colonel, a son to the late Brigadier General Vincent Homeboy, who served directly under General Douglas MacArthur. Mother had met this man a couple of times at the club she had been going to the last couple of weekends.

He happened to be the guitarist in a local band called "Stinger," playing music at Bay Area clubs.

His family was part of the Central Intelligence Agency and, for the most part, Romello only spoke to his family about his father's involvement in the Vietnam War.

All I know is that when we visited his family's mansion in Palmetto, Florida, it was like landing in a war zone: we were not allowed to talk; we could not leave the couch.

Answering questions began and ended with "sir, yes, sir" or "sir, no, sir." Romello was brutal, commanding a five-year-old like an adult soldier. The colonel was highly recommended in the ways of piloting helicopters, flying priority missions for the Central Intelligence Agency during the Vietnam conflict. This is all true.

Romello was very stern in his beliefs when it came to our chores. I guess he felt it was his responsibility to teach us that a routine included daily beatings, and properly arranged room's remains spiritually uplifting. If the beds were not made with pressed military corners, then we were punished with two or three lashings. Toys not put in their proper place and neatly arranged earned two or three lashings. At the age of eight and five respectively, Alan and I had to live with the fear of savage and brutal beatings. So vicious, that the point of sitting down let alone using the restroom, both were impossible tasks.

Romello had gotten a hold of one of our arms, his leather belt in the other hand; the sound of that belt sliced through the air lifted us off our feet and out of our shoes, screaming with terrors of this torture. I don't think our feet ever hit the ground until the punishments were over. Even the neighbors could hear our screams.

I don't know where Romello came from. He told us that his father was extremely strict and that he never was his father's favorite son. Romello was the youngest and weakest of the Homeboys' children.

That was hard for us to believe when every time, almost daily, he must have thought of Babe Ruth when he swung that belt against our bodies as he was trying to instill in us discipline. We were juveniles with fragile hearts. I did not know why or for what reason we were beaten. It felt as if we were sitting on a patch of sandspurs after every round of torture, our living hell.

Who was there protecting us from the mental and psychological abuse? When it came to her sons and husbands, Mother was blinded about the abuse. She lived with blinders on. We were young men with brittle hearts. Why did no one stand up for us? Romello preferred not to injure his hand. Instead, he readjusted our backs with a guitar strap or with his father's leather belt.

Manual labor was not a request; it was a command. We pulled weeds, lifted bricks, carried loads of wood from his car to the woodshop. We traded our youth in exchange for cheap labor, like the slaves of Egypt—made to labor in the hot jungles of Florida for this man.

Every day after the yard work, he performed an inspection of our rooms detailed to his particular taste, the chores must be made militarily, or we then get a taste of his beatings. This went on for almost a year, without Mother knowing the severity of the beatings, it was breaking our spirits.

The beatings caused a nervous condition with me; they created a second stomach in my intestine, making it impossible to use the toilet without bleeding from my rectum, as if he had bent me over to rape me of my youth.

It was not until my father married a woman named Savannah that they discovered the kind of torture we were experiencing. One night, getting into the showers, Alan and I looked like two Irish pub fighters straight from a backyard brawl. Our butts looked as if a truck had hit us, bruised from the meat of the thighs to the small of our backs. We even had trouble lifting our legs to get into the shower.

Savannah came in to give us fresh towels, when she saw our backsides, her mouth dropped open. The only thing she could do was yell for my father.

My father came rushing into the shower. We stood covering ourselves with towels, ashamed to show him what happened to us. Father asked us to turn around to show him our wounds. The bruises were in the exact shape of a belt; anyone could tell that a lunatic caused a blood vessel to break in two-inch patterns crossing our backs.

My father's expression said it all: the silence before his murderous rage, the temptation to grab his shovel to bury that cracker six feet under.

My father bent down to his knees, asking us what it was that we did to deserve that type of punishment.

We explained the chores he made us do daily, the unloading of the wood out of the old green Camaro, raking the backyard of any fallen debris. The pulling of weeds in both front and rear yards, with such attention to detail that absolutely no trash was found on the property.

Later that night at Savannah's house, there were loud noises, whispers, and strongly voiced opinions coming from the master bedroom.

We were treated like princes in her home. It was the only place I felt 'normal' other than at my Grandmother Clara's. Sunday was always the scariest day—we held our breaths as we traveled back home where we were defenseless and unprotected.

Savannah and Dad had concluded that these beatings must stop, or they would call the cops. As soon as we arrived at the house, we raced inside the backyard gates as we climbed the tree overlooking the side yard where Mom, Savannah, and Dad were standing. They were talking with one another.

We listened into the muffled sounds of their voices. Mother was saying that Romello had the right to discipline us, and she had no problems with the punishments.

That is when my father stated that if Romello were to lay another hand on us, causing bruises or any other marks because of his discipline, then he would notify the police.

Adrenaline flooded my mother with rage as she remembered the terrible beatings she endured at the hands of my father. She tilted her chin, centered her body, cocked her arm back, and unloaded her fist right in the face of my father. She caused him to stumble back a few feet. Dad looked down into his hands, spitting blood from his mouth and muttering words of retribution.

Nevertheless, Savannah took up for my mother. She warned him, "If you lay one finger on her, then I'll be the next to knock you out." As they left, Savannah blew us a kiss, saying, "See you kids next weekend."

My mother finally looked at Friday's beatings— now two days old. They were so bad it looked like we were still bleeding. Astonished by the sheer size of the wounds, Mother was appalled. The look on her face told us that someone was about to get exactly what Dad just got.

Romello arrived at the house in his old green Camaro we use to call the roach coach, now sitting on the side of the road. We held our breaths, this time waiting to see what our mother might do.

Romello walked in the door, sat down on his favorite lounger, and began watching television. Mother sat us down on the couch while she stood in front of Romello, blocking his view of the television. Romello began to complain, which just incited mother's anger even more. Without hesitation, she confronted him with it: "How hard do you think you need to hit my boys?"

Romello replied to Mother's allegation by denying the beatings, then asking to see our bruises. "The only thing you are going to see is blood dripping from your nose." Mother asked us to pull our pants down, showing Romello how severe the beatings were.

Romello looked over the markings on our backs, buttocks, and thighs, all he could say was that he was sorry if he hurt us. Romello told us that the punishment was fitting the offense, that our story about how the toys got under our beds was not the truth.

He said that he had only hit us four or five times. The smile on his face sickened me. He apologized again to us, saying that if we had not lied to him, we could have played with our friends instead of the punishments. Mother told him that if one more mark made its way to us, she was going to beat him with his own guitar strap.

Romello did it again, two weeks later. I had taken his grandfather's antique billiard stick and tried to chop a tree down with it. That pool cue was a one-of-a-kind Babushka, and I shattered it into a million pieces.

It was the only time I believe I deserved punishment, and he did not hold back. I took off running toward the front gate. Romello reached me as I opened the door, and he gave me the beating of my life. I tried to apologize for what I had done.

Romello dragged me to the scene of the crime to show me what was left of his grandfather's Babushka, scattered all over the backyard. I was young and confused because I did not understand why this pool stick was so special. Of course, my pleas fell upon deaf ears. Romello was a raging bull.

He brought me inside the house, dragged me up the staircase, laid me again across my bed, and then removed his belt from around his waist. Tears were already rolling down my cheeks as I anticipated the beating to come. I was praying to God to take this punishment from me.

I did not want to feel the pain of another beating. My backside had not healed from the last beatings. He proceeded to beat the life out of me. I tried counting the number of times the strap hit the back of my body. Leather cut through my flesh. My head was getting faint, and I almost blacked out completely.

He lost control, and I lost count after ten intense lashings. I was hurt badly, but my heart was also broken. The bleeding would not stop. I did not dare move. Nevertheless, I could not stand up anyway.

Luckily, my father was picking us up in the next hour. I was freed from fearing men for a day or two. Father pulled up outside the gates in the Thunderbird, Alan and I got in the car. As I fastened myself into the seat (I could hardly breathe sitting there holding my breath), I was barely able to sit up straight. I sat silently.

My father asked, "What's wrong? Aren't you happy to see me?" I said nothing. We arrived at Savannah's house. Later that night as we were eating dinner, she asked if everything was all right. I had hardly spoken a single word all evening.

Tears started rolling down my face, and then I started crying hysterically. Savannah took me aside, gave me a big hug. She asked me again what was wrong. I had little control over myself, not having enough breath to say what it was that happened to me earlier that day.

Suddenly the courage came. The words flowed out.

"Romello beat me again today!" I could not stop the tears from falling on this wonderful woman's blouse. She laid me down in bed as I explained what I had done.

Dad came over to find out what was wrong.

Savannah did not want to upset me with the possibility of my father's anger. She laid me down in my bed. She laid her hands upon my back, cooling the wounds, restoring energy back to my soul, filling my heart with some much-needed love. As she kissed me good night, she swore that those beatings would never happen again.

The rest of the weekend was fine. I had gotten some of my spirit back by the second day. I feared the trip back home. I sat in the backseat of the car, quiet, not saying much, refusing to look anywhere other than my shoes. As we pulled up to our two-story colonial-style house with the wraparound porch, my stomach knotted up with fear. My father asked us to stay in the car while he went and had a talk with Romello, who was looking at us from across the front yard.

Dad was ready to give Romello the same kind of attention that he had given to my mother. As my father crossed the front of the car, he started to remove his belt heading toward Romello, who was continuing his work in the front yard. Father took a couple of large steps as he hurdled the fence, ripping his shirt off (his muscles were huge).

Romello started backpedaling, knowing this was an angry aggressive male ready to unleash a world of hurt upon him. As Father got closer, Romello tripped over a pile of wood, and he began to crawl toward steps to the porch leading to the front door.

My father started beating him with his belt, cutting marks on the inside of Romello's neck, arms, and back. Romello cried at first, but then the only sounds were of the belt smacking flesh and hitting bones. The beating lasted several minutes.

After that, Father proceeded to explain; "Now this is a man beating a man, not a man beating a child." My father finished Romello's beating with a stern kick to his upper lip, sending Romello spitting blood all over the front doorstep.

My father said that if one more beating took place; it was going to be the time and place of his own execution. Romello was as white as a sheet, his face covered with dirt and blood. You could see the holes Dad had cut into his shirt. Large red belt marks had been absorbed by Romello's flesh and welts covered his body.

Father turned to Savannah, and it seemed to me that day that his body was as large as a mountain. They both got into the car and returned to Tampa. As we walked up to the house, Romello began to clean the dirt and blood off his chest and face. He did not say a word to us. He retired into the house while Alan and I sat on underneath the large oak trees and waited for Mother to return home.

I was afraid that Romello was going to seek retribution for telling my father or further punish us for the harm that I had done to his favorite pool cue. Vengeance outweighed my overpowering fear that my father's anger must have taught him some manners. A couple of years went by, and the beatings never took place again. Meanwhile, my mother enrolled us in martial arts classes.

Savannah decided to divorce my father, leaving me again with missing pieces in my life. She was a loving, tender woman. All I wanted was someone to love us. It seemed that within six short years, the world was full of nothing but pain and agony.

I began to conclude that Satan was real, and that God was dead. This thought, purely ignorant, concluded until after my next encounter with death, the death of a loved one, and an eye-opening experience that left me gifted for the rest of my life.

I lost all love and faith that God even existed from an adolescent grudge over the loss of my grandmother. She meant college, a proper upbringing, and loyalty to God. My brother and I kept in touch with Savannah; I continued talking to her on the phone long after she and my father separated. Still, my life was not out of harm's way.

CHAPTER 4

The Oracle

My grandmother Clara was diagnosed with lung cancer. Within six months, she had become too weak to stand. I believe the doctors did all they could to save her life. She seemed to be preparing her final departure. She was amazing.

Day after day, she withstood the pain, struggling to her feet if she possibly could. She persevered by faith. When reality seemed grim, she kept a positive attitude. She was fearless because of her faith in Jesus. She read her bible, and she prayed.

She got better for a while, but in the end, she lost her battle with cancer. She never lost in the battle between her faith and fear, though. I clearly remember the day that my grandmother's life was stolen from us.

We were working at my mother's ceramic shop when it happened. It was a hot summer evening. Mother and Grandmother Clara were busy with their chores. Alan and I played on the floor at the front of shop close to the entrance.

Mother was in the back-painting lamps with the air compressor running. Grandmother Clara was working in the front of the shop, pouring molds, and keeping a close eye on us boys when a man entered our shop.

Alan and I looked up at him. He asked our grandmother if he could use the restroom. She tried her best to be nice to him; however, the restroom was not for public use. I think she suddenly realized that he was looking at her purse, and she tried to reach it, but it was too late. They both struggled for it, but the stranger was too strong, and he started to run away with it. He ran into my grandmother in the process, knocking her down to the ground.

Running through the front door around the building, he was in full sprint as my aging, ailing grandmother jumped to her feet and soared out the door in relentless pursuit. Her purse contained cash and, more importantly, medication.

She gave chase over five city blocks before her body gave out, collapsing on the side of the road. Her heart was pounding, and the chemotherapy that withered and poisoned her body was now only seconds from stopping her heart.

Her body was twitching as her heart started an erythema. Her face turned blue. Her wig lay beside her body as the thief fled, not aware of just how much he had stolen from us that day.

Clara was undoubtedly surrounded by Angels of Light who were ready to carry her up and away to Heaven where her palace waited. I have no doubt in my mind that she is now among the saints where she belongs. I wanted her here with me, of course. I felt her spirit separate from my soul just briefly.

The police were called. The ambulance showed up as they tried to help my grandmother. I remember very little about the rest of that day. She returned home from the hospital that night while Alan and I were scheduled to spend the weekend with our father.

That night I had nightmares about men hurting the ones I loved. These thoughts were darkening my dreams, filling me with fear, overwhelming my heart with worry. I was crushed, frightened to death. I was six years old, and I had just lost my dearest friend, my source of great love and comfort.

My brother and I cried. I could not understand why God hated me. I cursed God. I did not believe that He loved me or that He stood for anything other than death. I wanted my grandmother back. She was gone, and nothing made sense.

Father tried to explain that her spirit was instilled within our souls, that God collected all her images that illuminated her aura with her eternal flame that reflects her presence in eternity.

At the house, I saw many people standing in a crowd on the front lawn. I saw my mother stepping out from the front door, holding Grandmother Clara's Holy Bible in her hand.

Her cheeks were swollen; her face blood red, her eyes pale blue, black stripes of makeup were flowing down her face. *How could Grandma Clara be dead?* Before Mother had a chance to see us standing there, she reared back, and with all her might she threw the bible from the house, saying that she could not believe in that scripture. Due to her lack of faith, she cast her salvation aside.

The bible landed across from where I stood. As it turned out, it became my father's burden, his duty, to stand that cross upright. Father picked up that Holy Bible, with his thick calloused hands. He walked up to the front door as he dusted off the pages. Placing that book under his arms, he began to smile as he remembered the place where he used to be known as a man who binged on belief the way an alcoholic binged on booze. My mother embraced us for a moment and then returned to her room to cry herself to sleep.

Days later, the time came for us to make our peace. We were to say our good-byes to this wonderful woman we loved very much. The funeral home was filled from top to bottom with lilies and roses. Many wondrous colorful bouquets of flowers surrounded her casket.

I started to make my way toward her lifeless body. I peered over the edge of the casket, looking down on her face. She was covered in makeup. I felt her hand; she was as cold as ice. I refused to believe that she was not there. I could see her. She had to be sleeping! I refused to believe that she was not coming home anymore.

Mother was finding it difficult to accept her mother's death even more than we did. I remember her managing to say, "She had more in this life to accomplish. God had no right to take her!" Overwhelmed with grief, I leaned over and gave my grandmother a kiss. Her skin was cold, like granite, and her scent was no longer there.

I returned to the back of the viewing room and began to weep. At such an early age, I had become aware of the purpose for my grandmother's death but argued the facts.

They chose Alan to read her eulogy, 'Footprints,' as I was only seven years old and could hardly read.

Later they cremated her body, spreading her ashes among her most favorite places in the world: The U.S. Virgin Islands, Saint Croix, and Saint Thomas, and around the garden at home.

After my grandmother's death, the fact was that I, too, had many experiences with death. I remember the first time I could recall witnessing someone else's death and the transformation from earthly presence to the spiritual realm. I remember the night I saw my first ghost.

I was asleep in the back of my mother's new Chevy van when a loud crash and bright flashing lights awakened me. Sparks lit the jungle and smoke quickly filled the air. I jumped to my feet, wiping the cobwebs from my eyes.

There was a bright glow radiating from the back and black shadows surrounding the fire. Bright cylindrical lights illuminated the back windows of the van. My mother slammed on the brakes right in the middle of Park St. and Elbow Lane.

She jumped out of the car to survey the damage of the accident. I could smell the smoke billowing from the truck that had lost control, snapping a power pole in half. The power lines fell on the truck. Sparks came from the wires, contacting the truck.

Meanwhile, my mother was helping to pull one of the occupants out of the burning vehicle. She went back for the second occupant, and I started to open the door to get a closer look at what was going on.

I began taking my first step outside the van to digest the casualty and devastation. Through the smoke, I saw two men outstretched on the lawn. They were lying on their backs, the first one covered in blood, crying, and concerned for his beloved friend's well-being.

The other man was grabbing at his legs as if they were broken. The steam and smoke billowed out from underneath the engine as a small fire had begun to grow. I can distinctly remember both men lying side by side on the grass.

The driver appeared thrown from out of the truck. He rolled around on the ground, flailing his arms as if he was in hysteria, grabbing at his legs.

During the chaos, the passenger sat and cried uncontrollably, with blood dripping from his brow. The driver's blood drenched clothes were almost shimmering off his black leather jacket. He was laying there with a gaping hole in the center of his chest, gasping for air as if he was an asthma patient.

Apparently, the force of the accident had thrown the man out of the truck directly on the grass in front of where I stood. The truck wrapped around the utility pole. It did not take long for the police to arrive. Shortly after they got the power shut off, they quickly regained control over the situation.

My mother was frantically crying, as I looked down at the person gasping for breath. I could see his eyes rolling in the back of his head. The driver began to transform.

The driver started to dissipate into the fog as his spirit started to leave the aura of his soul—bright pinks and purples. It was as though his spirit was presently here on earth, yet his soul had started to separate from his body.

My mother came up screaming for me to return to the van as I vacantly stared into the fog where this driver once lay. He smiled at me. I saw him reach out for something as his spirit was entering the light.

My mother turned me around moments before I saw the image of the driver once again, this time standing next to me dawning the colors of light, taking his first steps up the gateway into Heaven.

I was seven years old, shaking due to exhaustion and the cold morning air. I looked at him in disbelief. I then saw his spirit one last time. Looking deeper into the truck, I could see that the driver never exited the vehicle.

The driver was killed on impact, his head laying back, his mouth gaping open, the large motor of that truck sitting in his lap. Yet I had witnessed and almost spoken to the individual outside the vehicle as his spirit led away from his body.

At seven years of age, I tried to describe to Mother that I had seen the dead person outside of the vehicle, that his presence was transformed within the moments of his departure.

Others did not see this. The officer shuffled me into the back of my mother's van. He covered up Alan and me with our blankets, not wanting us to see any more of that accident than we absolutely had to witness.

I learned that morning that life is fragile—as fragile as a child's spirit once it is beaten and broken. I realized that my anger escalated because of the abuse. My soul filled with a seed that grew into hate, fear, anger, or shame. Without a clear understanding of God's presence, His love dies in the heart, unprotected like a rose withering in the hot desert sun.

Because of my grandmother's death, my grandfather started to take extra painkillers. Yet the emotional pain was nothing compared to what his medication was preparing to do to his mind.

I recall the night (I was no older than seven years old). My mother had pulled up to his apartment. Alan and I got out, looking forward to the candy snacks that our Pop pop had stored in his cupboards.

We walked up to see that his sliding door was open, and the apartment ransacked. I could see that Pop pop was lying in a pool of blood. My mother started to scream. This was too soon after Grandma's death to lose Grandpa!

I was again witnessing life at its final stages. I don't believe my grandfather intended to take his own life. He was a brilliant man. He was one of the few pathologists in the medical field to study the brain of Albert Einstein at the Steadman Clinic located in Trenton, New Jersey, in 1954, under the supervision of Dr. Thomas Harvey. Where my grandfather Dr. Brown took one vile of Albert Einstein's plasma home and administered the plasma to his wife, children and then turned the IV drip on himself. Like, some mad scientist he kept the secret until he confessed to one of his children. Who told me the whole family had large amounts of Einstein's DNA in our genetics.

My mother and brother had to run upstairs to call for an ambulance. I knelt next to my grandfather, watching his life slip away with every passing second. I was alone, holding his artery closed. I did not want my grandfather to bleed to death. Kneeling beside him on the kitchen floor, I was afraid for my grandfather's life.

Pop pop started to talk about what caused his cut on his leg. He began to tell me that Nomads, a secret agency of evil spirits, had broken in and torn his house apart, causing him to fall and cut himself on broken glass. I held my hand underneath his thigh. The blood was pumping out all over the floor.

He started to speak, asking me if I could see them: the shadows lurking around each corner. I turned around. My answer was that, yes, I could see the shadows moving. I was very young, but I remember the blurred images of the shadows he described.

They were surrounding him as I tried my best to stop the bleeding, screaming for my mother and brother to return. After that the ambulance arrived, and it carted my grandfather away. Not long after that, he slipped into a coma and left this earth. After years of fighting his addictions, while witnessing things not seen by the common person finally left this place and joined my grandmother.

CHAPTER 5

The Dream

Darkness plagued my thoughts, like a fungus covering the jungle's trees. I found myself alone again with unadulterated judgments. Ferocity and torment were the results of my awaking dreams. Each dream always started with an angel's voice calling for me, deep within the courtyard.

As it was in the song, "Bring Me to Life" by Evanescence, "It seemed my spirit was sleeping somewhere cold," as if it had stayed out all night until dawn, with my feet dirty from the night before. The covers were pulled over my head. Night after night, I had heard strange voices calling me, as if something was encouraging me to join in.

Every night I had the same dream. It was as if something was drawing me to the angel's presence. The fog blocked all sight of view; the opaque mist filled each dream. Night after night the fog lifted make it possible to distinguish what it was that required my presence on those dreadful eves.

On the seventh night, the moon was as bright as ten thousand lanterns, giving off enough light as the sun, making it easier to distinguish what it was that brought me beyond the boundaries of our home. An angel of darkness was sitting there, as if he was perched on a branch. He did not look back at me, yet he was waiting for me to join him.

I could see that there was movement in the backyard like silhouettes or shadows of animals, figures, and people running in circles. He sat there watching them with an empty blank stare. His eyes were like staring into a tunnel that light could never pierce; the emptiness of those eyes told me that there was a presence with no soul. His eyes were empty; the darkness that filled them was like peering into a vast void where nothing good could roam. I tried not following Satan was drawing me to his presence.

I sat down next to this dark cloaked angel of darkness, squatting on the deck. He placed his arm around my shoulders saying, "It sure is nice to seize you again." He asked, wondering, "Why is your fate returning to me? I have secrets to tell."

At that moment, I saw a blue flame erupt from Satan's hands, as shadows surrounded this fire, as if they too were a part of the blazing blue flame. Then he collapsed into himself, left a dark void where his presence vanished. He reappeared and started to whisper words into my ear that I could not understand. They sounded as though they were the echoes of a forbidden language.

Then the angel of darkness said that he knew all there was to know about my life. He said he had to watch over me to make sure that no harm fell upon me, just more of his lies.

I could feel his tongue gliding in and around the inner lobes of my ear. He said this was the last time where I had gained the advantage by seeing him weakened by his interest in me, but it wasn't. Then he moved away and returned. The daylight was breaking, he said, "I have one last thing to reveal before my presence and my energy ceases to exist. You might be the one. However, you will not know what this gift that makes you so special to us. Slowly, until then, bide your time until that time becomes your solution."

I was then able to use God's power to harness my energy, providing good news that brings forth the Lamb, as His light dawns upon my tabletops. It was time for the rooster to crow. I looked back toward the open door to our house and turned around again to see that the angel in the dark cloak was gone.

The Angels of Light stayed close to ensure the bargain was made, the covenant was bet, and the promise of prophecies was to be my life's story to tell. I remember.

Gabriel's smile in all his and her beauty (All Angels can be both male and female at any given moment).

The four Angels sent by God each had a name and a purpose. One was a record keeper (Derdekea), another had foresight (Raphael), then there was my guardian angel (Michael), and behind him was his protector (Gabriel).

The only things left were the shadows that appeared to be bird-like. From out of the darkness, the angel of darkness surrounded us with fire. Then behold four celestial beings speaking in tongues. They were chanting a song that sent chills down my spine, freezing my heart. I feared my soul being pierced. I was terrified.

The sonic boom created by the collapse of Satan's presence caused a chain reaction that caused my heart to stop and the evil of this world to begin entering my mind through thoughts and reactions. That precipitated the hell to follow the fury of the fight deep inside my soul, a fight for survival, a battle of the fittest.

As I was sitting there in my pajamas, my mother grabbed me from behind, asking me what it was that I was doing out on the back deck so early in the morning. I told her, "I had a bad dream, and an angel of darkness asked me to sit beside him on the deck."

Mother implored and asked me, "What hallucinations are you having now, Shawn?" I explained, "He had something to give me. I sat with him outside."

Mother asked, "Who was he?"

"An angel of darkness called the Day Star." I announced, thinking of that first encounter with Satan the messenger.

As I shrugged my shoulder, I could tell she was losing her patience with me. "What was it?" Mother asked, digging for answers, and searching for the truth. "I don't know! It was a secret. I want to tell the truth! It was extremely cold. I can hardly remember his words," I replied.

Mother brought me back inside the house. She asked, "Was the angel there? Or was it in fact a man in your dreams, a part of your brain not quite awake?" I could not answer her questions. I still had much to learn. I wanted to know how to express one's inner thoughts.

I had the premonition that somewhere inside the blue blazing light was the secret behind life and death. I know that angel was evil. I could smell the stench of death, like moths, on his clothes. He was there to secure his power over me by placing wagers, casting lots, consenting to covenants about how strong I could be.

He scoffed at the thought that I could be a strong adversary. His search would last for eighteen years before I had come across the presence that Satan saved from the clutches of hell to battle a force like me.

I spoke to only one person about these dreams, about the angel of darkness dressed in black. Although not always visible to the naked eye, his presence and energy made it easy to determine when those angels were nearby.

It was not a feeling of comfort, yet the uncertainty of fear overpowered by my curiosity. I wanted to read that angel's mind while returning to God's people the answer to their strife.

I spoke to my father's estranged wife when it came down to the Holy Bible or the laws of Moses. Savannah was a maiden—in many ways a prophetess herself, a witness with much insight—with the ability to predict the future, to teach what elements are necessary for prophecy.

I told Savannah about these dreams since she had told me that she was once a white priestess who had many battles with witches of different covens. For most of her life, she had been a student of Catholic ideology.

I thought she might have a solution to this mystery, an explanation of the dark presence I had encountered. Savannah explained to me that it was most likely a bad movie scaring my faith, captured glimpses of my grandmother reaching for me beyond the grave to help me.

I asked her, "What about this blessing of supernatural sight? For what reason, does Jesus need me to convey His messages? Why was it a secret? What kind of gift could the Lord Jesus Christ need to defeat Satan, the father of lies? Destroying the rest of Satan's fleeing angels back into the darkness with nowhere else to hide?"

Savannah replied, "This gift will help you discover when God is ready to use you! You will be powerful indeed. That I know. What this gift will do begins with the exploration of your mind. You will discover this when it will be the right time for you to use it.

For some reason God's intention is to keep that secret from you now, the gift is a secret to protect you from yourself. You are not far from danger, yet Jesus Christ is a sentry, a sharpshooter, able to spot any enemy that could come your way. He will protect you."

She then said a prayer for me over the phone. She stated that these dreams did not have the power to instill fear in me; she said to sleep soundly. I was trying to forget all things said by that nightwalker, that collector of souls.

I was uncertain whether this gift was from God or a curse from Satan. I laid my head to rest after that conversation with Savannah. She was right. I ceased having dreams, no more mysterious angels of darkness or witches speaking to me in tongues. No more rogue angels chasing me through foggy woodland jungles like Prada.

Now my dreams were occurring when my eyes were open, like peering through panes of stained glass. I was beginning to see the light emitted by the spirits that surrounded me. Then they began to speak.

It was not until several years later when I had found out what this secret was about, how God and His Angels of Light intended for me to use this gift. The knowledge of these celestial sightings turned out to be no curse, yet I was uncertain how to use it. To heighten my sense of awareness preparing me for battle, this gift was destined to change my life.

I watched for the moment those angels of darkness would return to me. This time it was no dream. God and His Angels of Light needed my senses acute to capture the purpose for Satan's master plan.

After Jesus Christ return, there will be a second war in Heaven, as a legion of son and father, mother, and daughter, will fight the final attempt to overthrow Heaven. Just lay hands on your opponent and walk through them. Every angel will be recruited to battle then only the worst will oppose us.

Satan had one purpose for his visit down in Florida. He would relieve me of my burden, taking my life in the process. While in meditation, I was absorbing the information that radiated from his mind. I gathered stories about his revolution, how they conspired to fool the world. By the end of this manuscript, you will also see their master plan.

He almost succeeded—if not for the communication and eternal bond I had with my grandmothers, Savannah, and the love I had found for Jesus Christ, I would have been lost. He had spent all those years preparing me for the time I needed to have the absolute and strongest will.

A decade and a half later, a demon left me in the depths of a mental breakdown that gave me bouts of foresight that I had not had before. With these abilities, I could see visions while perceiving thoughts through white noise an additional sense like telepathy, telekinesis, clairvoyance, and high intelligence. Predicting future events like the earthquake and reactor meltdown in Japan in 2011, then the Presidential race in 2016. To determine actions and events before the incidents could take place. I don't think Satan thought I had survived, and yet I did. I came out with a better understanding of the abilities blessing me with additional senses.

Once I started to fight for myself, the struggle became too great; the life that I had worked for and treasured immensely was something I had to release to God. It takes several years of battling demons, lost souls, even Satan himself to become a true warrior of God.

By that time, before the forces of evil had a chance to finish me, I had successfully barricaded myself inside a structure with no walls, without windows to look through, absolutely no doors to exit from this hell. My body was stripped to bare bones, with everything I had held dear in my life, even my sanity put into question.

All I had left was some clothes, my unconditional love, my proverbial heart, and a couple of pieces of scratch paper explaining what went wrong in my life. What happened that made this father of three write this tell all book about my insights and beliefs? I am not sure how else to write. I must explain what has happened to bring us to the turn of events that has you reading my manuscript again, today.

I was drowning, and somehow, I survived by some miracle. I fought the good fight! Jesus dispatched me against the forces that had attached themselves to me. Like leeches, they sucked the marrow from my bones, leaving me with absolutely nothing to fight for other than Jesus, my family and humankind.

My faith, my ability to love, God's everlasting forgiveness was all I carried deep within my heart. After all, how else can anyone explain the fact that I survived? The angels of darkness could not stop themselves from trying to kill me.

CHAPTER 6

Don't Take the Girl

This chapter is about a group of Boca Ceiga High School Pirates located in my second home Gulfport, Florida. We just couldn't wait for graduation, so David and I grabbed two Gulfport native sisters and ran to the shore where our love blossomed into four beautiful children.

I can remember the day when I met this bogie medical magnet freshman; she became the absolute air that I breathed. The static electricity created when I touched her skin. How I longed to kiss her and feel her touch. She was the presence of peace; I was extremely lucky to have found her at such an early age.

I can remember her scent, sending my hormones out of control, by calming my troubled spirit, removing the boulders from my stomach. I was not at peace with the world until I met this wonderful and courageous young woman: named Josephine.

With her jet-black hair cut shoulder length, her eyes pierced my very soul. The moment I walked into the room, I glanced over my shoulder to see if this girl would soon become betrothed to me. She brought meaning to my life. She was my constant sunshine, even on the rainiest days. I noticed that she was perfectly arranged. Too young to have that much grace, her innocence was like watching a star being born.

I was accustomed to dating girls much older than her, ones who had been hardened by love's pain or scarred by lovers' bites. I felt as if real love was knocking on my door. Everything inside my head said, "Leave this girl alone, and go to college."

I was trying to tell my hormones to let her go. Everything that made her perfect, made this girl perfect for me. God's lessons are ones that any and every poor soul should have to endure—that his love is a blessing.

The fruits of our lives are created by the choices we make. That mountain that turns to the sea is the words that have been misspoken. They cannot be taken back. Choose wisely before you speak.

If I could change one thing about my life, it would be to speak kinder words. I should start by surrendering myself by expressing my deepest sympathy and great regret for the unspoken kind of words that should have blossomed love and endured freedom. I besiege your forgiveness and desire your mind penetrated, your heart overwhelmed. Justice is in God's time; seek shelter and she shall be found. Hold tight your lips, knowing that only one was sinless.

Don't complain, make good on your promises, stand and be righteous while facing your fears, overcome your doubts. You should learn from other's mistakes, assuring that you don't fall into the same pit yourself.

Something about Josephine's presence brought me memories of adolescent dreams and desires. I had a dream that foreordained our union, uniting us as a pair. She was the last good thing that brought a smile to my face.

Josephine was a wonderful person. She will forever be my mate. Not quite a soul mate, yet she deserved the illuminations of a crystal chandelier hanging over the entrance to her Heavenly home. Bright lights shine down on her from Heaven, where darkness has no place to hide. Josephine was my greatest misfortune, who to this day still loves. I am here on earth now correcting my mistakes before I go see the Heavenly Father, judged for all to see.

As I stand naked, ripped open to ridicule, bearing what scars Jesus Christ bore for me, he then will shield me as a cloak. His skin shall become mine, we will occupy the same space, and it will be a time of celebration for the new sun shall dawn.

I will walk the steps of my Heavenly Father, claiming the name proclaimed to me while turning to my queen, looking through the eyes of her Father, turning out the lights before we go to sleep. That is when the night dawns, the stars will brighten, and another galaxy will be made.

Two of the purest of hearts cast throughout the galaxy, dreams illuminate the darkness deep within your mind as your heart longs for the moment you find your soul mate. Once those two souls meet, that star will ignite, and Heaven shall shine throughout the darkness forever.

Josephine was as cute and cuddly as a church mouse at such an early age. I did not know that she had a dark side. I believe her Cherokee blood gave her no consciousness of fear, absolutely no thought before entering battle! Not to forget we were a group of Bogie Pirates.

She was, like many in the Cherokee tribe, predominantly raising strong women who would die to save those they loved. She had a great capacity for love. Her heart was what made the difference in our relationship. Full of passion, her strength was what was lacking in my life. I wanted an assertive, genuinely caring female.

A week went by, and David (my best friend) called me to ask if I wanted to go surfing. The answer was always yes; the only question was, "When are you going to pick me up?"

David pulled up in his father's van, decorated with Boca Ceiga graduation graffiti. David's van had a nice, comfortable bed for a backseat. I stuck my board in and went to sit down. Much to my surprise, there she was staring back at me. She had her hair pulled back with navy blue and gold ribbons, lavender-colored lipstick and emerald, green eyes.

I played it cool. I talked to David while looking at her. I wondered what it was that she had going on in that gorgeous mind. At the beach, Josephine and her sister Marcy laid out under the sun. David and I began our jog down the shoreline. By the time we finished the race, I was trying my best to catch my breath. She was trying her best to ignore me.

I refused to let this girl go on ignoring me. I decided to sit down next to her to strike up a conversation. I was not going to sit there having her pass me off. I was a charming, kindhearted young man. I did not play games. I loved the female form. Josephine body was radiant. Her lips were like sweet cotton candy. She was irresistible to me.

David and I began to surf a bit while the sharks maintained their distance offshore. When we finished with a couple of sets of surfing, I positioned myself right next to Josephine, I was looking for what it was that made this girl seem irresistible to me.

I asked, "Are you enjoying yourself?" With her crooked little smile, she said, "Watching your wipeouts was extremely entertaining." I asked, "You like to see men get hurt?" She replied, "No, but I did enjoy watching you fall!" My curiosity was piqued. I asked, "Are you in a committed relationship?"

Shrugging her shoulders, she replied with, "Not really, my boyfriend left for the University of Alabama, I have not heard anything from him in a month."

My intention was to capture this girl's interest for myself while trying not to think about this girl's age or why we should not fall in love. We talked until the absence of light turned vast and void of any illumination. The conversation was about friends, the future, our passions in life, the things we loved, and the treasures we missed. The conversation came easily. It flowed as smoothly as that magical starlit night.

Looking back on the time we spent together, I know that God's presence was not far from us. There was to be a lot of beauty to come from this union and an abundance of love. In order to get to Eden, we first had to go through hell and the evil mob waiting to block our emancipation.

We made plans for the following weekend. There was a big funfest on Pass-a-Grille beach. A local radio station was throwing a major party. It was going to be the place to be. Disc jockeys, Sea Bass and Marla Stone, were hosting a skim-boarding contest. It was a who-is-who and a best dressed to attend. Josephine agreed to meet me out there.

This day was one of the all-time greatest days of my life. It felt as if this day of fun in the sun lasted ten thousand millennia. The skim-boarding competition was the opening event of the day's festivities. Bogie with several other schools were representing that day. Many events took place that morning.

There was the water-wrestling contest, where the men bear the women upon their shoulders, and the last couple standing wins. There was the building of human pyramids and, of course, the hotdog-eating contest, where my brother, Richard, placed first, eating twenty-two dogs.

Josephine arrived shortly after the second heat. I was cutting through the waves with more intensity, with a hot new Michael Dobley board giving me the edge on the competition. We exchanged glances throughout the course of the contest; her smile drove me to turn and burn, cutting that board harder than I had ever cut before.

I placed second out of forty-five competitors. It looked as if I had placed first in this young woman's heart. I walked with her down the beach, holding her hand, our feet at the edge of a cliff. The water was cold, but the emotions were hot—and this was only our second date.

We enjoyed the rest of the day together, I rather enjoyed her bathing suit in that hot, sticky weather. She was not excited about the saltwater; when we entered the ocean, she latched on tight with her legs wrapping around my waist, her arms locked around my neck.

Our lips close to touching not more than seconds from that first kiss. We were teasing each other as each wave pressed her body tighter and tighter to my own. Arms caressing her hips, she leaned in. Our eyes closed, both our tongues exploring the pleasures of making out.

Pressing and holding tightly together, we drew back, looking in each other's eyes. We embraced. We enjoyed the moments of raw passion; the serenity overtaking our bodies, euphoria accompanied us the entire day.

Her presence was like pure oxygen to me, her beauty like an illusion, her touch like the skin between us, the static electricity tingling receptors in our brains, our bodies absorbing each electrical shock given off by every beat of our pounding hearts.

The tall cliffs pinned our bodies between the rocks and the ocean when our two souls became one and our love was greater than the sea. In that moment, I found peace living within me. In our strongest moments, our souls were eternally compatible.

After the torture of the first fifteen years of my life, I felt as if my spirit was visiting a different universe. Wrapped up in this Angel's arms for an eternity was where I thought I wanted to be.

My adversaries were in search of destroying anything I held dear. They were hell-bent on the destruction of hope, the loathing in the chaos, fear, and misery. They had been on my scent for years, long before I was born. I held tight to Josephine, praying this love would not die like so many other great things in my life.

Nothing lasts forever except life in eternity, and this day was not over yet. After building our human pyramid with our friends the Plum trees, with Josephine placed on top. We hung out with Sea Bass and Marla Stone, and waited until it got dark.

I was entering the tenth-grade year of high school, though it felt like college to me. I had just turned sixteen, and I was stricken with fear that I had gotten Josephine pregnant. Months went by.

This secret, and our fears, plagued our hearts and minds. We made our decision and agreed that the best solution was to allow the baby to be born. We kept the secret for over five months to abolish any chances of an abortion.

We were at the edge of those cliffs, holding close to each other. The rocks were sharp; we were terrified. The fear was not death by the glaciers below, but rather the consequences of our indiscretions. Informing our parents was what worried us the most.

Life was not turning out the way I had intended. What else was I to do? I was absent of rational thoughts. It was time that I swallowed my medicine, to think about others over myself. This teenager was getting ready to have our first Angel. It was almost more than I could bear. Three beautiful children were created from this union.

I had bought the house my grandmother owned when I was a child located in Jungle Prada. Therefore, that is where the story picks up speed.

I started my own air conditioning company by the age of twenty-one and added another 1,500 square feet to the house. Business was good, life was perfect, and somehow, we decided to allow drugs into our life. It started with marijuana, then it escaladed from there.

CHAPTER 7

The Illusion of Sin

Warning:
The following sections describe a time in my life that included drug use and sexual behavior. As such, it is not meant to be read by young children or anyone who may be offended. I am apologizing in advance.

My intention is to tell the truth—which includes decisions that brought evil close enough for me to witness. I am not proud and the truth hurts; I need to get this off my chest. The moment I let drugs and alcohol into my life, Satan came to disguise my true intentions under a web of deceit.

"To open their eyes so that they may turn away from darkness to the light, away from the power of Satan and to God. Then their sins can be forgiven, and they can have a place with those people who have been made holy by believing in me." – Acts 26:18 NCV

I was about to take a dive into our cesspool.

Our vanity living inside us was the beast waiting to get out. It had been seven long years of working twelve-hour days. It was time for us to take a break. The family was in place. The key was to find new ways of experiencing life on the beaches of Jungle Prada.

Josephine was willing to harvest a habit that her mother frequently indulged, usually in dark corners of the house. We were about to venture into hell by something as seemingly innocent as smoking marijuana.

I was bound, captured, soon to be led to be slaughtered, like that of a fallen calf ready to worship any idol. We prepared ourselves in the mirrors for the night's festivities of dancing, partying, and sexual interludes—led by the laughter of a perverse plan put in place long before I was born, for my achievements meant nothing.

Those achievements were thrown into the air the second we decided to let drugs into our life. I did not have the strength to resist the sexual advancements and the drugs.

Everything was great, except for Josephine's mother. Roberta's resentment had brought our family down. Aside from Roberta's drug addictions, her pride had grown as strong as her jealousy toward me.

She was responsible for setting the trap, pulling the strings of her own daughter. She was envious. Her actions and her words reflected her intolerable hatred toward me.

We excluded her from our son's birth, and she was hell-bent on securing her authority over us once again. She had made a spectacle of herself at the birth of our final child. With her illegal drugs was the determining factor on how she extracted her ultimate revenge.

I'd like to think that she had have treated me as a son, yet she treated me like a blue tick coonhound, lazy as the day I was born, unfit to provide for her daughter.

Josephine was no longer in control of her decision making. Since Roberta once proclaimed herself to be god, she must have thought she had control over all things in the universe. There was no controlling Josephine or me. We were two young spirits that never had a home until we built one, never had a glimpse of adolescence until we discovered some reasons to act like idiots.

The summer was hot. The romance was reaching new peaks. The boundaries were about two young vibrant parents with difficult decisions in a quite complicated life. I will not lie. I had promised Josephine a better life then her childhood provided, and that I was deeply in love with her. We were inseparable and passionate. We had a unique sense of togetherness that must have stemmed from us marrying at such a young age.

Now that Josephine had turned twenty, and I, twenty-two, Josephine became restless and wanted to go out to the clubs. I agreed. Josephine was bisexual and wanted to find women to bring into our bed.

Please don't stop reading. This is my testimony. What hides in the darkness has seen a great light! I repented, atoned, and sought salvation to pay it forward; to bless the weak, sick, hungry, thirsty, and poor, to give their life a chance to increase their wisdom, and knowledge. To fill your life with love, harmony, laughter, happiness, a promise that eternal life is our goal.

Josephine and her mother had always been active users of marijuana and other hallucinogens. Josephine and I were eager to purchase the drug to experience the sexual side effects.

Although the sexual effects were fun, I am almost certain that when you use drugs, you take God's glory out of the equation and allow Satan to slither like a serpent beneath your bed sheets. Neither you nor your mate is at the bow or stern of your vessel, tied at center mass, tossed upon the sea without anchor.

I was not fully aware due to my youth that God ordains people with visions, dreams, and insights of the promises that we too shall live forever. Filled with vanity, fear, and shame due to our sinful situation, I comprehend the gift God intended for me.

I watched Josephine and Gwen dancing with several other girls, caressing, and kissing each other. Our sins called lust, our habits were drugs, and our lessons were constant rituals of ungodliness.

Yet, Jesus Christ our Lord ultimately forgives us. I perpetually atone, worship and repent! He protected our family when His spirit came to me in prayer. I could see His presence. He is real the moment you begin to pray. Either His spirit is near, or He is listening. On many occasions, I have witnessed His Holy Ghost.

I agreed to try that drug one last time. Josephine left to go to her mother's house to purchase a very big bag of piney green substance. As we smoked it, I was not accustomed to this black magic or the difference in an act of ignorance. I was overpowered by denial.

Little was I aware that our decision to smoke this misdirected tool of lust would lead us to the presence of evil and advance us in a dance with Satan.

Josephine and I walked many hours down that long road of perdition, deciding that our finality and reality could go hand in hand if only we knew to turn right to God.

Our case was that we were walking down that road most traveled, a crazy cocktail of drugs and alcohol, while licking the fingertips of Satan. When he barked, we'd bow, puke, and pray to make it through another day.

As all the excitement began to climax, the stars started to fall. The music was the rhyme between us. The heat was the friction of our burning skin and making love with her was an intensely enjoyable sensation that lasted several hours.

Josephine and I both pondered inviting another into our sexual excursions, as it would multiply our orgasms. This is how we came to meet a girl at a downtown nightclub called Janus Landing. Clothing drenched, saturated with perspiration, our heartbeats' bass, the percussion from the drums, every man at the bar gazed at me dancing with two beautiful women. My adolescent juvenile friends wondered what it was we had in our pockets that night.

The faithful father and the hopelessly fertile mother danced the night away with Gwen, our *au pair* whom we had met while at Janus Landing. We were on the dance floor; the girls' temperatures were rising. They were on the verge of ripping each other's clothes off.

Salt crystals collect from my perspiration percolating from my pores, streams of sweat cascades from my brow to my chin. I ordered and drank another couple of shots of Absolute Mandarin Vodka and Red Bacardi Rum. As my mouth filled up with those burning citrus flavors, I let myself explore Gwen's wonderfully tight body as she grabbed at my endowments.

I knew that she was not my wife. The presence of the devil took over, as she ravished me from behind the neck. She forced her tongue down my throat in a quest to absorb those last remaining drops of rum, titillating my tonsils as she sucked the last bit of stale breath from my chest.

The lights were spinning. The floor was jumping, and the drug Ecstasy, placed upon my fingertips. Our brains were rolling, our hearts throbbing as our lips bled from savage biting kisses.

Customers at the bar were watching us—us three, nearly adult dancers, performing as if in a public fantasy— the rolling of music, the blindness of our beauty. All were wondering what it was we had in our pockets that evening. Bullion rolls and rolls of gold bullion to give to the poor and needy.

A limo was waiting for us outside the door. We got in, asking the driver to take us home. On the journey, back to our castle, the silk was the skin between us as our flesh began to burn. Cooked alive, our bodies prepared to be fed upon by a demon sent by Satan to terrorize my mind.

Instead of going home, we drove the town crazy, the girls flashing their festive evening gowns. The lights were down, my body was pumping adrenalin. My thoughts were not for the weary at heart. We were not living with God. I was a disgrace, for God's presence was nowhere near us. Our presence had descended into a dark vat only Satan could enter, enjoying the pleasures of our pain.

All that surrounded us was the chance that Satan needed not to succumb for he had already entered this dance taken over by his barbaric music. That is when he started foraging for us from beneath the sheets. If only I had the chance, I'd have run out of that house butt naked. I was not within reach of a rational mind with both women in my bed.

For the next ten hours, it was partner on top of partner as we bathed in each other's flesh. Like the night of my conception, we must have looked like pigs in a trough, rolling around naked, unrecognizable to Jesus because of our shame. We had been taken over somehow, deceived by Satan, commanded by death, manipulated by the devil.

I will not go into too many details about the sex and the drug use. Over the course of two weeks, I went from a loving father, devoted husband, and working-class hero to marijuana smoker, ecstasy roller, and philanderer.

I was ashamed. I was supposed to be the leader of the house. I took all the shame deep within myself. To hold all this guilt was what drove me to adolescent behavior, causing me to lose sight of my pride. Why should not I have fallen into the hands of Satan's angels?

A man who claimed he was a priest was to come and visit us. His name was Damion, and he was engaging in coitus with my sister-in-law, Marcy. I would discover that he was not who he said he was.

Now, with our sin, it was as if the spirit of my former self was thrown from Heaven's gate. God's ordainment was already dispatched many decades before he had arrived, knowing, and foreseeing the end of time.

Through my mouth with God's words, my actions bound by His will, my greatest victory shall be salvation that began with the cross and ended with the sacrificial lamb.

CHAPTER 8

The Ladder of Salvation

Now that my Achilles' heel had been severed, I was unable to run from my captors. The Lord Jesus Christ forgave my ignorance and sexual improprieties. Even though we had sinned, Jesus Christ's guidance had protected my family from the snares of the evil ones.

I was sleeping on our bed dreaming, even though it was not normal for me to dream. I was having nightmares constantly throughout my sleep, as though my eyes never closed. There were signs that a war was converging to my presence. The results of our actions had already set off a chain reaction that sent Satan's army hurrying on its way.

I was awakened by water droplets falling on my head. It felt as if gravity had reversed itself and I was sleeping on the ceiling, as the condensation fell from the floor, descending from a vat far beyond the underbelly of a keystone of lights, spinning around below us.

I spun over, rolling to the edge of the bed, my feet dangling over the side, touching the ceiling with my toes. My knees then hit the floor, as more water then landed on the broad of my back. I gazed upward and unfolded the answer to God's mystery. My ceiling had a leak, as a fracture caused a void that of an improper seal. My ship was already sinking.

Josephine rolled over in a stupor, mumbling, "What do you plan to do about this waterfront pavilion?"

With our sky literally falling right in the middle of our love chamber, the light started to dawn. The day was to be fruitful, and our nights spent with ease. I clambered upon the roof. It was old with rotten planks. The plan was to prepare for a new day.

As I stood on that roof, the rain drizzled down, mist surrounding the area. I felt euphoric. I know now this was because of the journey of Jesus Christ, who made His way to my doorstep before Satan had a chance.

Something was waking inside me. The worker bee was preparing to perform his duties while the drone prepared the colony for war. I prepared myself for warfare while Satan made ready his plan for war against me.

The battle of principalities was nearing, and the frontline was beginning in my living room. My thoughts bogged down with the guilt of the burden that we had placed upon ourselves, and in our hearts, we could not stop at this single act of indiscretion.

With the drugs controlling our thoughts, and our weakness being vanity, we had little control over stopping this violent storm that had already begun to erupt.

How could I do this to my family, to my wife? Even though she was a willing participant, it was morally wrong, and I was struggling with my conscious. This burden weighed on me. It was causing a moral dilemma within my spirit. I should have listened to God's commandments and avoided sin. My ass was already in hot water, and there was no getting out of the fire.

My brother and friends all came out to help me install my new roof, where there was a man among all men who turned out to be the symbol of all the endearments of Heaven.

He turned out to be the symbol of an embodiment of God's holy purpose. Filled with God's presence, his heart could do no wrong. Humankind mattered to this person. Loyalty, commitment, and honor were this man's forte. Jesus was the absolute of all brothers from the other side of the tracks.

His kindness was almost as overpowering as his ability to listen, outweighed by his passion for friendship. In the end, he was my greatest friend. He was to become my dearest brother whom I could look up to and admire. He took to my house as if a fish took to water and called it home. He was a pillar of strength lacking in my life for far too long.

Immediately Jesus and I befriended each other, as if he had always been watching over me since I was in infancy. He carried the symbol of a centaur that matched the signs of a spotter.

It appears he was always several steps behind me, disguising himself in the flesh of people's faces, looking throughout the images of their eyes, to ensure a serene environment. He stepped into our lives at such a time when the walls of my house were burning to the ground.

We were distraught over the sexually bad behavior and were full of repentance. I asked God, "Please help me stop this insanity!" Josephine's grandmother, Mrs. Billy Joel, paid us a visit while Gwen was crashed out in bed from the night before.

I don't know how it came about; however, Mrs. Billy Joel figured out that something was wrong. With me not being able to face her or look her in the eye, she knew I was ashamed of something.

What did she think? That the sexual activity did not include her great granddaughter? Mrs. Billy Joel sat there streaming with thoughts that I was the only guilty party in the house, that I had been playing Josephine as a careless hearted fool.

The first thing Mrs. Billy Joel did was run home to contact Roberta. That night, Roberta sent Satan on his course and with that woman's hatred toward me, there was no telling what consequences would unfold.

Roberta subsequently called Josephine later that night, asking prying questions about the beautiful *au pair* spending more time with us. Josephine told her that we met her at the club somewhere downtown.

She refrained from saying that she herself was the one who invited Gwen into the house, and that she was not only a guest at our house, but she was also a toy in our bed— this bed covered in scum. The stench was horrible. That bed did not even belong to us anymore. It was a stage of perverted acts that soon would sink me to the bottom of the ocean.

I was getting ready to get a lesson in the Wiccan religion, and my mother-in-law was sending two dark people with demons attached to their backs, sucking the life out of them while feeding upon souls.

Roberta had a premonition about what was happening behind the darkened circle of our eyes. She wanted more Intel. She asked Josephine if she could have her sister staying at our house for the week, long enough for her to exact her revenge. Josephine told her mother that Marcy should not be a problem.

Her sister had plans to spark our love nest ablaze. With her lies profound, her eyes vacant, deceit deep within her soul. I was struck with all this negative energy and was oblivious to this vacation until their arrival.

Roberta sent these two characters down to see what was happening in the privacy of my own dwelling, to snoop around and scheme up a plan of action to use against us.

Roberta was upset with the fact that we left her house unclean and disarrayed. That with her insane jealousy gave her the chance to unleash her revenge upon us.

First, she made a spectacle of herself at the delivery of our third and final child, Shelly, because she was high on drugs. Roberta's eternal condemnation of me stemmed from the day of our wedding. When the justice of peace declared, "If anyone had a problem with these two being wed, speak now," she did not speak. She held her peace. I wish she had said something then!

One late evening, as I drove through the jungle, I was pulling up to the house. From the looks of it, there was a bright yellow car parked in the driveway. Marcy had arrived from Indiana that night. I got out of my work truck, and as I entered the house, I could see Jennifer, my best friend's daughter. I was eager to see my old friend David.

As I walked into the house, I noticed that my bedroom door was closed; it was never closed except when we slept. I opened my bedroom door to see Marcy and some other person—not David—sleeping in our bed.

I searched the house for Josephine. She was preparing these students for their slumber party. I lay down on the floor to play with the young ones. That is when I asked, "Who is the stranger sleeping with Marcy in our room? Why are they in our bed? There are plenty places on the floor or the guest bedroom."

Josephine explained, "Marcy left David, and that person in the bed is Damion." At first, he asked to refer to him as Dominic. The truth is that Marcy had an affair with Damion, got pregnant, and was now hiding her firstborn from David, the adolescent's biological father. This sort of behavior ran constantly through Josephine's family.

Damion introduced himself to me right before dinner. I was not impressed. He was wearing satin trousers and button-down sleeved shirt with a clerical collar choking the blood from his brain.

We were trying our best to release ourselves from bondage and forgive ourselves for the temptation that we had been living.

We did have a moment of weakness and instants of confusions overheard by this priest. Damion's depth was far too great, serving Satan for far too long. Desiring nothing of God's redemption, he had plans to lead us further into darkness. Damion was a committed adulterer and claimed to have served the cloth as a priest.

Damion's study of witchcraft left the desire to seek true salvation, and the thought that Damion might be saved was out of the question.

Damion spoke constantly about his god, but really, his words were twisted. He could prey upon the house of the weak with his words from the "bible"—his knowledge of the black arts. This Christ saw through my eyes. Preoccupied, looking in the opposite direction, I had to find a place for him inside my home.

Damion's past was made known to me only after my walk to the water's edge. This priest reminded me of those shadows that sat before God's Angels the night of my dream.

When I found, myself awakened by a nightmare, he was in the backyard sitting on our wooden deck. He was continually singing that song, "Here's a little song from Heaven Angels sings / Bring glory and honor to where.

Calgary was slain / Hallelujah for the lamb that was slain." It was not so much the words, but his pitch and the tone that sent chills down my spine. He was mocking the Lord.

My three beautiful children were safely in their beds. Josephine was stoned, feeling absolutely nothing the moment that pill hit her stomach, causing her to pass out, leaving me alone in the darkness with Damion.

Marcy was likewise in that same dreamlike state. Screaming in her sleep, you could hear this once defiant youngster pestering God's redemption. Damion's soul was distracting her from God's prayers, with her sexual desires for Damion to return to her deep within her slumber. This priest was luring her far from the truth, while she beckoned Damion to return to her. She was undoubtedly a lost soul boldly defying God.

That is when it happened. He was causing events to turn our madness and sin into a bomb ready to explode. Damion was pondering my demise. The last moment of sleep, my mind clouded with a vision of Damion slipping into the master's bedroom, where Josephine and I lay completely unaware of the extent of his maniacal plan to overthrow my corporation.

Damion slipped past us with a white envelope filled with angel's dust. It was all part of the good father's plan to rid himself of my mind and take Josephine into his den to flay her heart. She could see the darkness of her delusions. Like Eden, the leaves were falling off our fig tree, and God was condemning me into hell for recognizing my nakedness.

Damion had overtaken my purpose, controlling my thoughts, encouraging my action with crooked teeth and his jaded smile. This demonic presence with his devilish art had his ropes like a curse around our necks, choking all the air from our lungs.

He had my sister-in-law, and now he wanted Josephine alone to serve as a tool of jealousy, to cause madness to set into our love.

As soon as our marital bed became unholy, Satan sent his demons directly in to devour, destroying all that I had. They were hoping to get lucky by killing me in the process, yet Jesus turned out to be too strong for that. I was stuck in a den with a viper ready to attack my withered body.

It was as though he had brought the stench of death's decomposing bodies, cluttering the floors with their corpses.

As Damion's demon saw more insanity, the stronger he became in holding my family hostage. Within the last couple of days of his stay, he fellowshipped at our church while having complete control over my actions, like some type of puppeteer. The house was busted; the bank was clean—even the power bill was on a three-day notice.

Damion was keeping me up nightly. The conversations were about God's creations of thermonuclear power, sins, and the effects that Satan could have in our lives if we were not living in the word of God. Due to the late hour, his words meant nothing. He was twisting the truth, souring his own testimony.

For the next six nights, this priest provided the drugs we smoked, the words that I debated, laying his hands on me almost every night, praying to God to steal my soul. I could not believe how sinister the way his words churned.

It was my family that lay in that foxhole, and I had to start running for cover. I was overtaken by guilt. My actions were calculated with measured steps. I was being led straight into a death trap by some mystic force.

CHAPTER 9

Abraham's Bosom

We sat in our house, suffocating in the smell of decomposing, putrefied, fragmented pieces of human remain littering the walkway, the spirits of the dead not in actual form.

Our scent was drenched in that nauseating smell, every part of our body mauled as if some voracious dragon had spent hours licking our wounds, preparing us for his supper. He was now about to dine with us. This dragon had no plan of surrendering us over.

I lost sight of everything because I was not walking in accordance with God. I was not living within His grace, many shameful allegations made against me. Thus, far, I had married my high school sweetheart, built two beautiful homes, and started my own business, all by the age of twenty-two years old.

My body was all torn and tattered from the lack of sleep. The torture that my mind had upon my heart was due to my contempt and the presence of evil was now living inside me. Every morning for five days I would wake from my nights filled with terrors.

Damion's constant conversation caused my conscious mind to wander throughout the darkness. I was walking through the terrain of a steep embankment, large cliffs with no trees in sight, to stop the winds from picking up sand, sending those small coarse granules stinging my face and eyes.

For five nights, something plagued my dreams. The spirits of my relatives were grief-stricken. I could sense their concern. The conversations again with Damion seemed to be endless. The smoking of marijuana seemed not to stop.

I was staying up all night, swinging on the front deck with his presence beside me, while Satan's spirits were not far out of hearing range. He was praising his soldier, for their plans were falling into place.

Although, I had work planned the next morning, even if I had to lay myself to rest, this man's words thundered unsure thoughts of anger with sinister moments of jealousy. He knew that my weakness was Josephine, and he aimed to exploit her. I was far too exhausted to see the trap he had placed in my path. These nightmares were far too real.

That next morning, Jesus was front and center with my complimentary cup of coffee. He was a genuine friend. He voiced his concern, seeing that I looked terrible, "Hey, boss, man, what's going on? You look like hell!"

I began to speak about the situation. I was alarmed with the heightened sense of evil, the darkness due to this stranger who had come down from Indiana. God only knows why Damion was visiting us, plaguing my dreams, tearing my soul apart.

Tonight, was the night I left Jesus behind in those next brief moments, I had a new perspective on the purposes God intended for my life.

I discovered many of life's mysteries occurring during another near-death experience. Both were about to happen at the hands of a demonic man. Damion tuned in with Satan's plan; was fully aware of the devastation, he was willing to participate.

Jesus was starting to gather the missing pieces to this jigsaw puzzle. It was his observation, "Damion sounds like nothing good could come from knowing him, and you look like you are in some kind of trouble."

I agreed with Jesus. I canceled the day of work and suspended all conversations with the priest. I needed to return home to get some much-needed rest. My plan was for us to go fishing later that night. I returned home to make love to Josephine while the sun was shining.

I walked slowly through the front door, exhausted. The guests were all off at Grandmother Joel's house. My children were quietly sleeping. God destined them for great achievements; God blessed those young ones. No one other than my children and Josephine remained inside the house while we were in such need of one-on-one attention.

Making love to Josephine that afternoon, I could see the contours of her obscurities. Ever changing with each fragile fraction, her eyes seemed to say there were mysteries hidden within the depths of her soul.

This secret caused me to wonder, adding that much more to my plate. There was fear, shame, and sorrow. Something was visibly wrong; the children could sense it. Shelly was acting out and constantly crying.

In the twilight of Josephine's eyes, the light started to dim, as if the essence of love captured that day on the beach was lost. My soul mate had been swallowed by the sea while the rocks below grinded those precious pearls into fine grains of sand.

Satan's warrior lay dormant, sleeping every night in the spare room, ready to unleash a plan against me. Suddenly my mind was without reason. Fears instilled into Josephine's heart by Damion implored Josephine to run away from my arms, out of the structure of our home to find refuge in the arms of her wicked mother.

The children came running into the bedroom, jumping on the waterbed, trying to arouse the restless lion from my much-needed slumber. I held Lora to my left and Shelly under my right, while Xavier rested himself upon my chest. Their love for me was everlasting, and their desire for my affection remains in my soul today.

We were playing, laughing, and enjoying the summertime until Damion walked into the room. What I did not know was that he had a joint laced with PCP in his pocket. We sent the kids off to the playroom. As Damion fired up that toxic joint, I was unaware of the angel's dust. I prepared myself for a journey that sent my mind to places I have never seen before.

The discussion of that night was about fishing. It seemed everyone was ready to cast a hook upon some bait to see if they could catch a bigger fish—they pictured stirring the tops of the water, drawing the pole down, sending the line in a hurry in the opposite direction. Damion was hoping for a one-on-one fishing trip with the two of us. My plans were already set for Jesus to go. Damion was more than welcome to go fishing, yet he refused.

The sheer size of Jesus had Damion on guard. I guess that frightened him into staying home to accost Josephine with his sultry words, in obedience to his covenant with Satan's desires. Damion once conveyed to me that he could see and hear into the hearts and minds of the Lord's most sacred people. He said he could read my mind and predict my future. That is funny; so, can I.

The moon was bright, and we were looking for some good fishing with the high humidity a thunderstorm began to bear down on our horizon. Josephine was fighting with her emotions that I should stay home, rest, and save the fight for another night. I was exhausted with not more than a few hours of solid sleep the prior six nights. I was on the verge of delirium.

I wanted to experience the technique of how evil operated, to attempt to devour all that is good, feeding off our sins, causing chaos, plaguing our sight, giving us an understanding of darkness. I was uncertain about the future.

These demons cast doubt within my mind, leading me to believe that Josephine had been unfaithful, sending me into a fit of jealousy, tearing down the walls of the very house that I had built.

From out of the darkness of the jungle, a little Toyota pickup truck pulled up in front of the house. It was Jesus ready to go fishing, for the night was full and the moon was blazing. The boat was ready to go racing with the stars.

The brightness of the planets that night was as if my sun never set. As we mounted the boat to the truck, I latched myself on to Josephine one last time. I did not feel comfortable leaving her with Damion, but he was adamant that he wasn't getting on the boat with Jesus.

The sun was setting by the time we got the boat into that clear water. You could hear the boiling of the ocean's currents beyond our horizons. The gray sky exploded with radiant pastel colors, streaks of white clouds casting shadows in the sky as the sun hit the ocean's floor.

I started to fall apart with apprehension as the drug raced through my bloodstream, wondering if Jesus's plan had the intentions of murder. I believe those thoughts were deliberately planted by a very diabolical man.

The sun was diving down into the depths while Heaven only knew what was to transpire next. The fact is that I almost ended my life by pointing the barrel of a gun under the bottom of my chin in a fit of rage. I was not planning to execute myself to make them see, that I meant every word. Therefore, I accused Josephine of having a love affair.

I was glad that it was my life almost taken instead of the innocent ones. Josephine and Jesus were suddenly accused of foul play. Josephine and I were both in the same boat, figuratively speaking, back-to-back tied together while this demon sunk his teeth in, pulling my breastplates apart, to show the purity of my heart.

Damion was unaware he had a tremendous battle with a warrior far greater than he! Battle we did, only for me to gain more intelligence, for the war was about each memory, and each memory was a testimony for me.

At the edge of death was a gray maze that bedazzled Beelzebub. The maze I speak of is the devil's treasure box. On top of this mountain in the center of this labyrinth holds a chessboard. The complexity of this game was such that not one figure had been moved for hundreds upon thousands of millenniums.

With the images of Merlin, the master looks down, peering at two of his soldiers floating in the bay, waiting for his rook to move for that game to recommence. Satan was elusive. Merlin contemplated Satan's next move, and Merlin waited patiently for Satan to reappear for the chess pieces to mimic his moods.

I was half-mad with exhaustion, clinging to the helm of this boat, taking a moment to regain control over my facilities, dropping my mind into a mental neutral. I started to pray aloud, screaming to the Heavens in the middle of the bay.

The dark priest laid his hands upon my wife, invoking the spirit in her, removing all sanity in me. Damion was a master in witchcraft. I knew no other option other than to give in and pray for redemption.

Jesus was sitting in the front of the boat, much older than I was. He knew where this was heading. He came to place his hands on my shoulders, asking if it was a better idea to return to the safety of the house. I was far too unsure about returning to that shelter. I wanted that demonic person out of my home and away from my family.

I know the silhouette of our Heavenly Father was playing roles in my movies. I was struggling with the darkness that started with allowing Satan into our lives, under our bed and between our sheets. The darkness was far too dense for me to see God's Holy Spirit. As I have heard it said, rise and you shall be counted; fall and you will go to sleep.

I was begging that this ceremony was not happening. Josephine was battling in obscurity against Damion performing his dark ceremony, invoking her spirit, removing her innocence, filling her with the void that breeds contempt. He enticed Josephine's good nature to cast doubt into my mind. He fed off her spirit to gain control over my jealousy.

The boat launched out headed toward the middle of the bay. We were driving this vessel out beyond the horizon, pulling away from the dock, the vessel in full throttle. We were breaching through the waves and cruising faster than that wind could push us.

We passed by the boat ramp at Jungle Prada Park. Where the famous explorer Pánfilo de Narváez landed his enormous ships and celebrated the first Easter Holiday here on the North American Continent. We went as far as Boca Ciega Bay and Blind Pass Canal closer to my favorite fishing hole near the Don Cesar.

The captain of the boat maneuvered through the wake of the water splashing equally on both sides of the capsule, as phosphorescence illuminated this vessel. We gravitated toward a lunar abyss as though we were floating among the constellations. The captain and his first mate maneuvered past Orion, skipping beside Pisces, picking up an array of stars, casting light throughout the shadows of darkness, underneath our sky directly beneath our boat, Aquarius.

On top of this vessel, both brothers, like sons, rode that river of slick oil. Little did we know that a holy war had begun, battling over

Josephine's soul. Satan had sent his messenger into attempt to devour her sin but choked on her salvation.

We pulled in close to the mangroves inside a lagoon, while my thoughts were choking with the absolute danger of a reef shark that lurked ten feet below the surface of the water. Within fractions of a second, I had decided to open the beer cooler in the center of the captain's bench. I removed the alcoholic beverages from their resting place.

I then dropped both bag and six-pack over the rail, sending it traveling on its descent, ten feet to the bottom of the bay. A four-foot reef shark came out of the depths. The phosphorescence in the water caused the crystal blue sparkles on the edges of this shark's teeth to illuminate with the moon's light.

That moment that the shark attacked those bottles has forever burned its image in my mind. I jumped back in horror. "A shark attacked the bag of vodka bottles only a few feet from my hand!"

Jesus replied joking, "Yup, no kidding. He was probably thirsty. Is that all that is left on this boat to drink, because I am not about to drink saltwater?"

I had no reason for throwing those bottles overboard. I just knew I had to stop all sin from happening around me. Somehow, that meant no drinking, no smoking, and no more sexual love affairs.

I was the reason this person was visiting us. For what better reason would Damion have, but to have me sick and out of my mind? I was hanging on the last thread of hope. I ran for the hills and asked for the Lord Jesus Christ's blessings.

Nevertheless, Jesus' apostles were with us all along. Destiny allowed all this to happen. I turned the boat toward my favorite fishing hole, where we got out our fishing poles. The fishes were all swimming near the top of the water, basking in the moonlight, as we started to cast our lines. I started to relive the last couple of weeks in my mind.

I was having some peculiar feelings of jealousy taking shape inside my mind. I was beginning to think about one night that stuck out in my memory. It was a night when I had returned home late from my martial arts class. It was late, and I should have returned home two hours before I did because I was getting counsel from my Sensei.

I pulled into the driveway. The light in the kitchen was flickering. I could see Jesus trying to sleep on the couch. His breathing was heavier than normal; I paid no mind.

I walked into the master's bedroom, where Josephine was sleeping, with the waterbed bouncing up and down. I could tell her pulse was higher than it should be for someone quietly asleep. The room smelled like marijuana, and I was suspicious that she was using the darkness to try to hide something painful from me.

I thought nothing about it until that night, when I was fishing on the boat with Jesus. I could not get the thought out of my mind that possible foul play might have made its way inside my Josephine. As much as I didn't want to believe it, not all my thoughts can consider that foulmouthed beast, Damion, was attempting a deliverance of Josephine's soul.

Now my weakness was confusion. I started to think that Jesus had seduced Josephine, betraying our friendship. Some outside force must have brought on this delusion. I am sure that Josephine was faithful, but I could not control the thought from entering my mind.

The curiosity was causing the jealousy to gravitate toward insanity. I was exhausted from the last several nights; hence, the deprivation of sleep. I started viewing life from a different perspective. Damion admitted prior to my attempted suicide that he drugged me with angel's dust. He exhausted my mind and body forever a week until my mind became irrational.

These drugs were now controlling my mind by Damion this dark angel with his dust. He was striking fear into my soul; uncontrollable sinister thoughts were overtaking my mind filled with more visions of lust between Jesus and Josephine. The drug was way too powerful. God, I know I made a big mistake!

I was fighting extraordinary forces—Damion's demon that had his clutches upon us while I experienced a living hell, standing outside the protective spirit of the Lord Jesus Christ. How did I protect myself through these trials that God was placing in front of me?

With the abilities to predict evil's intent throughout the future of this world. I was to tell whom and how many would believe me? To use the power of the Holy Spirit, to lend a helping hand through prayer, to become that guiding light (called Gurus) in the continuing battle over our beloved Heavenly Father.

The battle raged on. We returned to the boat ramp, the moon blood red, the water vaporizing from the surface of the sea. Jesus was concerned to see his friend stressed out, to witness this father of three acting out of character.

I was a person whom he cared about, torn from the presence of God into a dungeon, where Damion was alive and worshiping Satan. Jesus stated that I needed to spend more time with Josephine instead of late nights at the dojo. This comment further propelled my thoughts into madness, filling my mind with jealousy and rage. I was festering in my insane thoughts.

Not that Jesus had been aware of what was going on inside my mind. Maybe he did, but he certainly did not know that Josephine was preyed upon that night.

At the house, Damion talked for many hours, explaining to Josephine in the audience of her sister, Marcy, that he was 'of the cloth,' removing her sins to cleanse our house of impurities.

Damion laid Josephine down in the middle of the spare bed in the guest room. Her head and shoulders rested slightly against the wall as Damion and Marcy faced each other. They started speaking in tongues for over an hour, praying over Josephine's body, listening to each other's lies, obeying their god Lucifer, as they fed off Josephine's energy. That demonic priest started to invoke Josephine's spirit.

This dark madness was explained to me after Damion and Marcy performed this ritual. Josephine consented to him since he commanded much power over her as she fell into unworthy hands. He then could perform a Bunsen burner trick that caused phosphorus to ignite from a waxy green substance placed by her sister close to the vaginal womb, causing a false test of pregnancy while perpetuating yeast to ferment. This was impossible I had a vasectomy, so the chances where she didn't get pregnant by me.

The smell was vile as if all that is ungodly lay dead beneath her womb. It was horrendous. The inserting of this seed was an act of witchcraft, causing a tide to flow throughout Josephine's womb, imploding her flower to a rotten stench that was not dying anytime soon.

This caused a nauseating urination smell to trail her for the next couple of weeks. While Josephine was struggling to remove the terrible aroma, I had beaten myself down by my emotional duress.

CHAPTER 10

Time Odyssey

I felt as if part of my innocence was gone forever, the wings of angels being broken like Pixy Sticks. I could feel the uncontrollable urge to purge my soul. It was as if my spirit overtaken by some dark musical dance orchestrated by the devil himself.

Backing the boat into the front yard, the driveway was lined up with a plethora of vehicles. I got out of my truck, walked straight up to the front door, and preceded past the living room to make my way to the master bedroom.

Josephine lay in comatose from the number of drugs she had been taking. She was also exhausted from the dark ceremony preyed upon her—this sweet Southern girl now placed face down in a sea of pillows.

Josephine's snoring sounded musical, tuned as a tightly stringed cello performed in a five-piece orchestra, while I was the finely tuned piano man and Damion as the Director of this well-orchestrated symphony.

We were entertaining this dance with Satan, and his spirit was coming from all sides, encumbering our every move. We were running headstrong directly into his trap, not fearing the consequences of our actions. Our thoughts had multiple minds of their own. I kneeled beside the bed where Josephine was sleeping. As I did this, she woke up, screaming, "I did not do it, it was not me!"

Surprised by that remark, I had not yet figured out all that had happened to this beautiful young girl. She was in a trance that intensified my insane jealous rage. I felt like charcoal was coursing through my veins, waiting for a spark to ignite my soul. I sent myself into the furnace of that redefining fire, wiping all my impurities clean, left to sit and smolder.

I quickly asked Josephine, "The night I was late returning home from the dojo, did you have a sexual affair with Jesus?" Her reply was, "What are you talking about?"

I wanted an answer, not a question. I asked her again,

"Did you sleep with Jesus while I was out at class that night?"

She sat up and asked, "Are you going crazy?"

I should have bound my jaws with bailing wire, yet. I replied, "I think I am losing my mind!" Six days without much sleep and a warm head of red hair, Damon's body lay perched on the edge of the bed in the spare room, breathing nothing, but contempt.

Josephine suddenly jumped out of bed, yelling for Jesus as he came running into the bedroom. She shouted out, "He thinks you and I had an affair!"

I was ashamed by the accusation that I had placed upon two people I loved and cared about very much. Yet the master of puppet tricks was playing on that stage inside my head, and my heart was a pincushion. Repeatedly those pins were driving further into my organ, causing a murmur in my heart to skip beats.

Jesus woke up to my allegations. His anger was fast, as if a hot cup of coffee poured upon his chest. I reached inside my dresser, and I took out my Glock .40 caliber pistol for my protection.

I ran into the bathroom as they closely followed. In my heart, I knew this seemed like an illusion, yet it felt very real. I was not extremely positive that God's will exonerates this potential act of insane homicide.

There was no light surrounding us. There in the house ministering with Satan was a Wiccan warlord, former priest, and admitted adulterer.

Helpless and confused, I wanted to believe that it was a nightmare as I jumped up on the hot tub that was in the master bathroom. Fearing my life was in danger, I placed the gun underneath my chin, threatening to pull the trigger if I did not hear a confession.

I started to scream louder, "I want to know the truth, and answer me, goddamn it, or I'll pull this trigger. Josephine, you know I will!"

Josephine and Jesus stood at the doorway of the master bathroom, absolutely astonished by my allegations. It was not my rational thought process. I was mad, close to losing my mind. I was living through another out-of-body experience.

I screamed once more, "The truth!" Josephine broke down crying. I could see in her eyes that she was not capable of adultery.

What a scumbag I was, forgive me for I was unaware of the angel's dust given to me, no doubt by the order of Roberta. Josephine proclaimed her innocence, "I swear on the life of all my children! For God's sake, what have you been smoking?"

The angel's dust, the marijuana, the exhaustion became too heavy of a burden; the yoke became too much weight, my back sprain from this immense load. They both denied any sexual improprieties. I believed them both, but my brain was halfway down the wrong track; there was no way of defusing this missile.

The reason was not registering in my mind due to the drugs given to me by Roberta's demon. Roberta, Marcy, and Damion's plan were for Josephine to see me crazy and delirious. That would have frightened the hell out of any person.

I was a part of the problem, but Josephine was the one who wanted the weed. Gwen had the ecstasy, and Damion brought the angel's dust. Within two weeks, I had a full-blown drug problem that opened windows in my mind, releasing the floodgates that allowed demons to replace God's grace.

I stood on that hot tub in the middle of the master bathroom controlled by darkness, and all I wanted to do was cry. Jesus calmly said, "This isn't going to happen, Shawn. Nothing ever happened. Put the gun down, please. I have seen this one too many times. You are not going to pull that trigger."

He was right. I placed the gun on the bed. I left the room in search of Damion. For some unknown reason, this priest was drawing me to his presence. Like those mysterious angels of darkness that came to visit me when I was a boy, promising me the world.

Jesus and Josephine unloaded the gun, removing the pistol out of my reach. Jesus and Josephine went outside to discuss what happened over a cigarette, while I sought after that demon.

With all the yelling and screaming, I was surprised to see that only one person was out of bed. It was Damion, standing in the darkness of the bedroom as though he knew that I had come searching for him. Why was I there? This individual was evil.

I knew he had controlling thoughts over my mind, spells over my heart. I knew that darkness surrounded him. This man, he was far too close to my mother-in-law to be a friend of mine. Sent to cause madness to set into my mind, Damion tried to force a catastrophe in my life right before the eyes of my family. I was lucky to have survived.

Damion was standing in the darkness, his arms outstretched with his palms facing upward. He was gaining control over something that I could not see, like an illusion. Damion was now in control of my world, no longer living in disguise, walking around the bodies of the blessed. Damion could see the dead, while standing among the living, he would have determined whether I was worthy of God's sacrifice.

Silently he had stood at the foot of the bed, waiting for hours, meditating on our every move. After invoking the spirit and gathered from Josephine what he needed, sending this otherwise calm father into frenzy, the leader of the household under some demonic spell, he calculated his revenge with precision. He stood at the foot of that bed.

I entered the room; he looked up at me, motionless and without uttering a sound. He raised his arms up higher in the air, turning his palms face down. He said in short, small words that seemed to emanate from underneath his breath, "It's high time you receive the word of God. Where have you been, Shawn?"

I felt like punching that bastard in the mouth, sending him packing back to Indiana. He placed his hands upon my shoulders. I asked him, "Do you have any idea what's been going on here tonight?" Damion, without blinking the black lashes of his eyes, spoke, "Yes, I know everything, and everything is under your control."

He talked as if his words came from the corner of the room, like a ventriloquist articulating his words from something unseen. He came up to me, mending my shoulders between his hands, replying, "You should rid yourself of this thief, this man you have come to know as Jesus. He will steal more from you than the property beneath your feet."

Weakened due to my exhaustion, I was ready to confess all that had happened to me in the bathroom. It was like watching my image in slow motion on a reel-to-reel home movie. Like déjà vu, as if what happened in the bathroom between Jesus and I had happened in a previous life. I could see the lights of video cameras behind Jesus and Josephine, recording me standing on the Jacuzzi, pointing that gun to my head.

It was not possible. The one thing that I remember about that night was when the Angels came to me on the back deck, telling me, "This is your only life; you get one chance to make it right."

With a long length of rope tied around my neck, I could hear my neck snap as I became like Judas! I failed by letting my family and friends see me at my weakest. Mentally and physically, I was experiencing extreme amounts of pain. Why was I on that path of sex, drugs, and darkened toils? Thus, far, I had built two beautiful homes, had a party of five, and started my own air-conditioning company all by the age of twenty-three, but because of that fall from grace, God took all my blessings away.

I could feel the length of rope tightening as Damion started drawing me close, as he released the slack from the line to relieve me of my last breath. I was not completely crazy, but I was on the edge of a nervous breakdown.

The fact of the matter was that I had to straighten out my thoughts. The only way I could accomplish this was to rid my house of impurities. I had one more day with Damion frolicking about the house.

I remember a drip from my nose as blood began to drop on the floor. Damion wiped the clot away from my upper lip, causing my skin to burn. Blood started to flow, droplets landing on the freshly laid carpet.

Pinching my nose, I started to walk calmly into the bathroom to look at this bloody mess covering my shirt. These events were not common occurrences. This was not normal. Damion was odd; something was unexplainable.

The fact was I was going mad. I had accused my wife and my best friend of having intercourse.

The course was set. I had to trim my sails, steady my rudder. I was without my anchor, my ship was out at sea, and the current was too swift to maneuver safely away from the crevasse. With my ship, out of control, I found myself trying to remove all obstacles from my path.

After the embarrassments, causing my pride to shrivel, I asked Jesus to give me a break until I could sort out my thoughts. Jesus was as usual empathetic and agreed. Because of the hell that I brought upon Jesus, I brought him to the nearest ATM machine and withdrew two weeks of severance pay.

I felt a massive loss of tissue missing from my heart the day of Jesus's absence. I was hurting the people I cared about deeply. My embarrassment was what caused shame to be placed upon my house.

How many mistakes can one person make within two weeks' time? Every corner I turned to be another question. It was simply the result of bad decision-making. I returned home to Jungle Prada to reunite with Josephine, asking for forgiveness for my reactions. It was no laughing matter. For me, the drugs had to stop!

I begged Josephine to return Damion to hell from where he came and immediately return to life as usual before our roof caved in on top of my head. I felt lower than a swine; this priest would try to disguise himself as, to hide his presence from God.

I returned to the house after dropping Jesus off at his apartment. Josephine was outside with Marcy, smoking another cigarette, a habit that she had been trying out the last couple of days.

It was morning. I had been up going on seven days straight without much sleep at all. At least, I don't remember sleeping. My daydreams and my nightmares happened, regardless of if my eyes were open or closed.

When I got to the house, the smell of them smoking sent me straight into the master bedroom, determined to break this cycle of drugs, followed closely by Josephine and her sister.

While inside, they followed me into the walk-in closet in the master bathroom. I finally made a command decision to rid ourselves of that drug, removing the bag of weed from its hiding place, headed straight for the toilet.

Both girls were screaming, horrified that I was throwing the weed in the water. They grabbed at my arms, hoping that I had not flushed what was the last bit of the marijuana we had down the drain. They attacked me like that shark earlier that morning, the one that almost bit my hand off. Josephine yelled at me, "What the hell, Shawn? That is the last bit of marijuana we had!"

"Good," I said, "that is about to bring down my house and you are sitting in it! Wake up, will you?" Josephine stood in front of me with that lit tobacco cigarette in the house I built, in the house that my grandmother passed away in, all due to a damned neurotoxin. Staring at her, I removed the cherry from that lit cigarette. I threw the rest into the toilet.

I had to let her know, "You need to stop this before you cannot control yourself. Please tell me where it is you think our life is heading. Can we stop it before it gets there?"

Josephine had no reply. I knew there were worse troubles around the corner.

That night I had trouble sleeping. I was climbing in and out of bed. Josephine oddly enough was comatose from the number of drugs she had taken. Normally, we could not figure out how to untangle our legs.

It was a short sleepless night, and I had work planned for the next morning. With less than seven hours of sleep in a seven-day period, I was exhausted. My body was out of energy.

My mind could not comprehend a logical thought given the circumstances—the fact that Damion had laced the marijuana and I had been unknowingly smoking angel's dust with that drug. I called off the work for the next several days. I must have known I was heading into uncharted waters.

CHAPTER 11

At the Water's Edge

I know this all sounds crazy. If you give me a chance within the next couple of chapters, I will deliver messages and explain great theories. Bear with me. This chapter describes the moment I had lost my mind, and Damion told Josephine to leave me.

Roberta's primary objective was to have Josephine see me having a nervous breakdown, due to the number of drugs they had me taking. To tell the truth, I don't blame, Josephine's departure from the marriage. We went through a lot that year.

It was only over the last three weeks when I had gone from a noble man to a drug abuser, and then I committed a major sin while I was on drugs. It was a sexual affair with a very beautiful girl, after she brought ecstasy to a party we were having.

The moment God stepped away from my presence was when Satan stepped forth and attempted to disguise my true intentions under a web of deceit. Jesus Christ was staying close, observing my detoxification, waiting for my sobriety.

Angel's dust was something I had never taken. I had only been smoking marijuana for two weeks, and the window was open for my mother-in-law to exact her revenge. A song called, "Everybody's Fool" by: Evanescence, "That summer I was lost in her lies. I know the truth now and you betrayed me."

It happened to be Josephine's birthday. Josephine and Marcy had plans to go to the beach that morning for a party.

However, I was in a state of hysteria. My eyes blurred from the lack of sleep, the amount of stress I was under, crippled me with anguish. Exhausted from the angel's dust Damion and I smoked, just him and me, he always had the joint laced with angel's dust. The other girls never smoked the joints Damion had prepared for him and me.

The kids were excited to go to the beach. They all begged me to call off work and accompany them. Josephine was emotionally agitated due to all that had happened the night before. We were loading up and preparing the family for a day at the beach.

We loaded the Ford Excursion, strapped all the youngsters in their seats, and checked the radio forecast to make sure that there were no storms coming. Marcy requested that she get a chance to drive Josephine's new vehicle. I was in no shape to argue about who was to drive.

Damion got into the passenger seat. I sat with Lora as we started the short drive to Fort Desoto's south beach. Damion was in control of the music, playing some of his personal favorites, such as techno, R & B, and 'Disco Duck.' He was making gestures with his hands, trying to control the tempo of the ride.

I started wondering who Jesus was. Where in the world had he gone since the night before? What was his position on all that had been going on in the last couple of hours? He was gone. I could not blame him if he never came back. Onward and upward—I guess that is what they say.

I had begun to have some moments of clarity. My thoughts were bouncing from visions to permutations, to outer body experiences. My soul was in one big circle of survival. I was walking down that valley filled with shadows, for death kept a tight grasp upon my shoulders. This demon played with my emotions, altering my mind's perception of events.

The children's eyes were vacant, their eyelids pasted to their foreheads, barely blinking at all. They looked hypnotized. Oddly enough, Josephine was ignoring me, looking for something off in the distance. My mind was at its boiling point. I felt the taste of metal in my mouth, like acid rolling down the back of my throat. I realized I had not been eating, just as I had not been sleeping.

We pulled into the parking lot at the Fort Desoto's beach. The youngsters started to unbuckle their safety belts. Everyone started exiting the vehicle into the radiant rays of the sun's light. The vision I had was the beginning of a thunderstorm billowing up on our horizon. This squall was gaining strength.

I had no control over my steps, as though they might have been predestined or predetermined that my feet should have fallen upon the same footprints long before my journey to the water's edge. This would lead me to my closest near-death experience.

I was having another out-of-body experience. I was witnessing myself as a very small boy. The viewpoint was about twenty meters in the sky above my head. I was toddling my way to the edge of a very busy thoroughfare, struggling to make my way through the soft silky sand. I stood up at the edge of this dull embankment, a steep bend in the road leaving a blind spot on the highway because of the sun.

I took my first stride on the blistery asphalt. By my third step, I saw a very large truck moving at a high rate of speed, unaware of this white-haired boy walking during this daydream. This was no dream; that truck was barreling down the highway.

The truck swerved to avoid my body, not wanting to inflict any harm on this vulnerable child that had wandered into the road. Josephine grabbed me by my arm, pulling me back, removing me from harm's way. The trucker passed by blowing on his foghorn while releasing his air brakes. He was then able to regain control.

I stumbled back down the dune while the children were in a trance. Shocked, befuddled, I did not understand what went wrong. Josephine ran up to me, not sure if what had happened the night before was a prelude to today's events.

Why were these events happening? Where they predestined measures to fall upon us that day? I know that my future was looking grim.

I walked past the Ford Excursion. I could hear Josephine yelling at the children, "Everyone, back in the truck. Your father has gone and lost his mind."

You see, the only two people smoking that angel's dust was the priest and me.

It was for the glory of God that these trails were placed before me. This is also the reason why not one person has ever been wounded because of my visions. I am not a dangerous person. I see things that normal people choose not to believe in. All my spiritual warriors served their purpose as I tried my best to serve my Lord Jesus Christ.

Headed toward the churning waters on the edges of the Gulf of Mexico and Tampa Bay, everyone was rushing to reload the van with Damion and my family. All I remember is Damion yelling, "We'll come back for you later."

With a cunning smile, he closed the door to the truck. Josephine threw the Excursion in reverse, leaving tread marks in the sand, alone without any comfort to me as I was abandoned by my family. I was not a boy. I wished she could have understood that I was the only person in danger. We were better off together instead of separated. She decided to leave me behind, sending me offshore on the verge of dying.

I could feel the presence of evil, like droppings of shit upon my shoulder. I fell to my knees and began to pray for God to intervene. My prayer was long and intentional. My fears were then comforted. The day's events had yet to determine the effect it had upon my marriage and the way my family viewed my sanity.

Marcy had notified the police of my condition and my emotional state of mind to get me arrested or to take me to a mental hospital. I was an unknown soldier of God. If you can bear the thought for a second, all that happened to me was for God's great purpose.

We conquer many enemies in the name of Christ our Lord, my brother ecclesiastically speaking; He is an inspiration of our inner self, a mirror image of perfection.

Ever since I made the mistake of taking those drugs, I had been sinning against God. I never forgot about my father, and who it was God intended I should be. He came to relieve us of our guilt and our burden while forgiving our sins. I was placed in the middle of this chaos to hear what it was that Satan desired the most, revealing his plan to control my life with his attempts to destroy humankind.

Under my coarse exterior, you will find one of the gentlest of creatures that God has forevermore ordained as one of the Lord Jesus Christ's Archangels, where I shall sit with my Heavenly Father. Determining the strength of my faith, you shall see why I may someday kneel before the throne in Heaven to stand at the right hand of God.

On my knees, I prayed in the center of the pathway. I prayed for clarity and guidance, the concrete cutting holes into my flesh. I was not aware that hundreds of insects had covered my body—the ants and mosquitoes drawn to my carbon dioxide, sweat, and perspirations of blood. The results of their anger were vast numbers of welts that covered portions of my arms, chest, and feet. I stood up knocking the mosquitoes off my body.

I looked to my left, and I saw a figure. The figure was of my father twenty-two years before that day. He was waiting for my brother, Alan, who came running out to him. They embraced.

Father picked up the two fishing poles with his left hand, grabbing Alan by his right hand, walking off, out, and around the sea oat burrow.

They were looking toward the setting sun sending its rays across the ocean's surface, causing the water to flow red with the tide. It was not a good day for fishing. Beyond a distance offshore, hundreds of angry sharks circled the reef in search of food, a vast number of bait fish swim pass the mouth of the bay headed out toward darker water.

What sounded like a gunshot rang out? I spun my head to the north in the direction of the blast. It was in the middle of a picnic party. I could see the smoke, visible, as students were running, scattering to the four corners of the parking lot.

I heard another gunshot as I walked up and over the table where Merlin had been marooned, sitting on that island. Merlin was contently playing a game of chess contemplating his next move. It had been Beelzebub's turn for the last ten thousand centuries, not a single chess piece moved until then.

This visible being had not yet released his bishop, refusing to give into this master of disguises. Merlin waited patiently for his opponent to return for the pieces to move again.

I passed over the top of that chess match in the presence of evil. The property of magnetism is that an opposite reacts with two poles conducting electricity. The instant Satan feels threatened, he reverses his polarity and repels from his opposition.

That day his interest was in my near death. Having no intention to finish the game until one of the chess pieces moved, Merlin yelled out, "Why, Beelzebub!"

Within four swift moves, Merlin had Satan laughing with Damion; all there was left to do was to devour my queen. Checkmate! Merlin slammed that last piece down on the table causing the tablet to increase in size exponentially.

Merlin had warned them, "You may take everything from the young man, but spare his life. He has insight and will write a book about all that has been presented to him."

Out of my own consciousness, left vulnerable under the spell of evil presently around me, I started my walk to the water's edge. Merlin rebuked Satan! Satan was befuddled that he had fallen into a trap. Merlin tried to convince him that I was far too old to be the one he was after. It had little effect. He knew who I was; the markings were upon my body, tattooed in ink.

I stood there at the water's edge, my heart banding a tune of deliverance. My heart was pumping with immense fear. I was not sure that I had to do to survive to save lives. That day was another step in a journey. I hoped that God might save me that day, and He did.

My mind was inside that windy tunnel of a hurricane, the gale force winds blowing like hell crashed down upon my sails. Brewing in turmoil outside my body was the perfect storm.

I took off my clothing to show I had no more shame. I walked myself into the water naked, splashing about without a care in the world other than reaching my destination (the other side of the bay).

The finish line was unknown to me, the purpose a secret. Shame for all the bad decisions we had made was what should have brought me home that day. Nevertheless, I was far too deep in the water to turn back now!

By now, the authorities had been searching for me for the past half hour. All the roads watched, and now the rangers had started their search of the beaches. Damion had my family under his rule; it was too early for him to leave. Returning home to Indiana without my death certificate was impossibility. I was swimming for my life in the surf. My prayers to God—surely, He must have heard my outcries.

I was left alone, so heavy in my sorrows. I was like a rock; my body having been hardened from the physical work I did and the martial arts training. Muscle is heavy, and I dropped to the bottom of the ocean.

I placed myself upon the sacrificial cross with no one present to save me from the hell that had been controlling my actions and thoughts. God's guidance was there in abundance, it allowed me to think I might make it to the other side of the bay. Swimming through the shallows, I could feel the organisms of the ocean sliding across my body parts as I swam naked through the surf.

I only opened my eyes when I heard a large object splashing the water close to my body. The wake of a moving school of fish caused ripples of water to come rolling over my head, sending water into my face, causing my eyes to open and burn with the salt of the ocean.

I looked forward as a large Tarpon rolled its enormous tail in front of my body, tunneling down to the depths below. I kept swimming deeper into the Skyway Channel.

The water brisk, the current swift, as my body began to drift toward the old Spanish Keys. My feet were no longer able to reach the ocean floor; the bottom was sixteen fathoms deep. I was two-thirds of a mile offshore, and a hundred meters from the last sandbar when I ventured out into open waters.

I took a deep breath. I rolled over my back, diving headfirst down to the bottom, where the light of the sun fades. I could see several objects circling my body.

Unbeknownst to me, I was surrounded by a large school of black tip and hammerhead sharks. I was taking my last moment to consider my fate when two large porpoises swam from behind my body. Like torpedoes, they passed me, and the rush of their wakes cast the sharks aside.

As God is my witness, they were sent for my protection. I was again pushing the envelope, testing my fate.

I was in danger, only God's spirit could save me.

At that moment I decided to swallow the saltwater that surrounded my submerged body. While I was inhaling the water that surrounded my body, I could hear the sea filling my lungs, until no more salt could fit into my collapsing cavities. I was losing consciousness.

My body began to shake and quiver. My eyes closed as I blacked out, my heartbeats slowing. All I could hear was Savannah's voice begging me to breathe. It took moments until I hit a window. An opportunity presented itself to save my life, for me to come back from the edges of death.

Face down in the water after a few seconds, with the saltwater in my lungs, I began puking violently, purging my lungs of that harsh vile liquid. Thank you, Almighty Jesus! With the sharks, not far from me, I started my journey back to the shore.

At that moment, I was alone on this planet; the sky had cracked open, I was too late to correct my mistakes. Everyone on the earth was taken, and it felt as though I was the only person left behind.

I started my journey back to the shore. By that time, the police and the park rangers sent a helicopter out to rescue me. There were far too many sharks in the water for the diver to enter in after me.

I swam to freedom as I saw my country's flag flying in the wind. Nobody was on the beach to see this son return from the sea that almost swallowed him whole. I was suffering from exhaustion and dehydration, looking for something to drink. I found my way to the ranger station to hydrate myself.

I walked up to the station nude and disoriented. I was not concerned about the fact that I was naked. Shame held no card within me, being delirious due to the amount of saltwater that I had digested.

Inside the ranger station, I passed the two females who were sitting to my right. They were soaking their feet in Epsom salts due to a stingray barb in her leg. I did not mean to scare them. I was delusional.

I started to drink from the fountain. The fluid was now coursing through my veins, diluting the saltwater in every major organ in my body.

After all my near-death experiences, this day was the day that I had come closest to ending my life. God and His Archangels, who were fighting several evil presences, surrounded me.

I might not have survived to tell my story. However, after this day, my mind was a tuning fork, receiving vibrations of both principalities battling over my soul!

The saltwater had my mind in a tunnel. I did not mean to cause a panic. I grabbed the keys on the table that belonged to the two women. I had to get home as fast as I could to cover my naked body. I wanted to find out if my family that I loved was home.

After they screamed, I dropped the keys on the floor where one young woman was now covering her eyes. The park rangers had started to surround me, blanketing me with a small crowd of people.

I was fighting my madness, as if my eyes had acquired a new ability to film these objects, to envision the shadows of people's spirits as a delayed reaction to movement. When I visualized my family members, the ones who were dead and gone, they were as real to me as the rangers.

The spirits were there, and their presences never left my sight from that day forward. They were not only visible; they had become audible. Pandora's Box was opened, and this gift was no longer a secret. Perhaps it was the saltwater or the fact that I was seconds from dying in the ocean. I was foaming from the mouth when they commanded that I lie on the floor. Then the sheriff placed handcuffs on my hands.

While walking out of that ranger station, it was the first time I had seen Josephine since she pulled me out of the middle of the road. She was standing in front of the ranger station crying hysterically. She was wondering what happened to her husband. Why was I behaving in this manner? My senses were heightened, my antennas were up. It was as though God had blessed me with the sight of these Angels, the Holy Spirit and Jesus Christ.

The doctors were trying to restore my sanity by relocating me to a medical clinic, where they placed me in four-point restraints. The saltwater was still deep within my tissues. The doctors gave me a shot of Thorazine as I begged them to remove the sin that left its tracks, tattooed like scriptures upon my body.

I had allowed myself to have these markings placed on me, as I heard before on my mother's side of the family that inking was a tradition, not just a family affair. I hear parts of my bloodline holding their judgments of that Native American tradition. These tattoos had become the distinguishing characteristics that can differentiate me from any other idiot without as much as a fingerprint. I was now recognizable to any fool labeling me as criminal.

I was lost in this world of visions that gave me the ability to see ghosts, figures of broken spirits, lost souls not yet committed to Heaven. It was when the sighting turned audible that this gift turned into a blessing from God.

CHAPTER 12

The Final Bow

For many years, I have been separated from my children (and, no, I was not in prison), and it took me over seven years to learn how to construct sentences with subjects, verbs, adjectives, nouns, prepositions, and pronouns. I found that redefining my inner self was like a new love interest.

Lora, my oldest daughter, was entering college by the time my book was ready to be studied. I was on the brink of superstardom, as I was preparing Xavier for manhood. I see Shelly in the center of her light—a brilliant girl searching for answers to a missing father she forgave.

I have only seen my children a handful of times. I take comfort in the fact that they are strong even without me in their presence. I enjoy the fact they hold their tears, living without fear in their hearts, hoping that I might return to them someday.

I was unable to work due to my on-again, off-again illness. I had some frightening experiences dealing with my spiritual sightings making me a powerful prophet.

What the doctors diagnosed as schizophrenia brought some very scary spirits close enough to me, that made me believe I was being followed by the government and watched over by demonic spirits. I have come to grips with this disorder. I have material witnesses that are not of this world that continue to visit me on multiple occasions.

It is not difficult to imagine that with my sight; I must have been born this way. The disorder is maintainable if you know how to stop the visions. I have decided that my descendants need my explanations of the importance of trying to uncover the truths behind Satan's curses.

I have made leaps and bounds with the way I have been treating these ailments. All I needed to refocus my thoughts was a local shot and a couple of well-prepared manuscripts.

I have made many mistakes: the early marriage, the drug issues, the arrests, the near-suicide attempts. I was sexually molested as a young boy, and it made me crave physical contact. With an absent father and a mother who abandoned me, I turned to sexual intercourse at the age of thirteen.

These things bring me to tears. However, I want to tell the truth. If I had lied about my circumstances, then that would make me a false prophet. The Lord's messages have caused me to repent, atone, and seek salvation.

I am in a safe environment now, although for a long time, there was death, chaos, and mayhem surrounding me. With the number of crimes in the streets—rape, murder, torture, abortion, and spousal abuse, not to forget child corruption—part of everyday life, it is too agonizing to sit and witness.

That is the reason why Angels hold people who live a righteous life in such high regard. Our decisions and choices are an act of free will. Angels are prioritized in their movements. They are calculated with measured steps that are as pertinent to their missions as subordinates. They guide the spirits of people close to death and fight battles over the demons that feed off fear and misery.

When these spirits came to us for help, they had evil presences attached to them. Sometimes these evil presences lash out and attack. I have seen many Angels that capture these evil presences and cast them into hell like rats.

Channeling, or speaking with spirits, shows me that there are far too many enemies in the world for God's spirit to handle alone. We must be worthy of battling our own inner demons to save each single father who was unfortunate enough to let his stove burn out in the middle of winter. We must keep the fire stoked hot enough to rekindle the love once lost when God's plan was to take his flame elsewhere.

To learn from these obstacles, I have found preserving sanity, myself battling over my inner demons to find Christians, Elders, and Holy Spirits watching over me.

If only the good ones in the government tried their best to turn the tides, preserving the light, the last storm that falls upon this earth should not be an atomic explosion. We must correct all the pollution problems and give life back to this violent planet. People wait either for the glory of God or for the prince of darkness. We must prepare to see the light through a complete operation of this machine purifying water.

Satan wants us to leave our children fatherless with careless mothers, unhappy in death, while life is left a mystery. I have never actually seen a murder. I have seen my own death, I have been close to death many times, yet I don't know how I will die.

I know that these inner pains hurt. I hope that someday my descendants know how much love there is for them in my heart. I fought for them as I slaved through the field of thermodynamics.

The children wish not to worry about the absence of their father. I know it is because of the distance. The pain is too much; they rather leave a void in their life than to fill it with pain.

I know that they will understand my beliefs and wish to read some of my writings. After all, these are my stories, and they are true. Perhaps, this is the truth only seen through the eyes of a mortal man. Nevertheless, I know they will understand that they are loved.

My bloodline held away from me due to my spiritual beliefs and my opinions, they don't realize that their genes contain genius and knowledge is not wisdom. Don't let others pull the wool over your eyes, because those who are deceiving are the same ones serving themselves over the Lord Jesus Christ.

I guess I shall wait until they are older to express the joy of my life to them, for now my visions occupy most my time. Lora, Xavier, and

Shelly you three are Supreme Angels now and always the greatest joy in my life.

When those children were born—Lora, Xavier, and Shelly—Heaven's gate opened, your souls descended to earth, and then Angels began to sing. Those words churn the very wind that makes the butter from our cups of cream with my children's happiness, as if recreating mountains straight out of molehills. With your every step with God makes your souls like lamps to guide our way.

You are made like the Lord Jesus Christ, a perfect image of an Angel with the presence of the Holy Spirit to be made useful in God's army. You serve as a warrior placed into a harness made with wings grafted from within your heart, a guiding light, forever a perfect illumination of grace.

If I had a chance to prove to my children how to become a son or daughter of an adoring God, it means that God must be present, and you must serve the Almighty Lord Jesus Christ's people alone, as well as with others.

When the day to be with the Heavenly Father comes at last, He shall anoint you, while appointing you over His houses as leaders in His Kingdom, all swearing allegiance to Jesus Christ. We shall each share trust in the twelve tribes of Israel, and then we shall be together, in Heaven, preparing for the festivities. I lay on my bed resting.

There is more than a great understanding to life after death. His secrets, like our inheritance, are held with all positions that are ready to be given to the few that make that greatest of effort, while keeping their covenant with God.

You rein command over the most desirable people to apply servitude to the Lord Jesus Christ patiently resting on His throne. To be more like the Lord Jesus Christ, you should accept that He is within your mind that He takes over our body and He needs our soul cleansed.

Nobody likes to sleep in dirty bedclothes; no one wants to walk around in someone else's soiled laundry. The same concept about your soul being cleansed, Jesus can't fill your body with the healing power of the Holy Spirit without your soul being cleansed.

The moment He decides to remove you from your position in Heaven, preparing you for more adventures is when you will blink, and He will be free to use you with His powers.

At your desire, you will be able to fly and dive off any mountaintop, and no harm shall fall upon your children who will be protected by all the Angels and forces of God across the universe.

I love you, Lora, Xavier, and Shelly. You are the hope that keeps me alive. Lora, you are my first Angel who changed the essence and direction of my life; you brought meaning to me, a promising child's existence. Earlier on in your life, when your mother and I began the process of sexuality with the pregnancy, as young as we were, I was commanded by God to be your father. Absent father though I was, I am sorry for that void that I hope to someday fill.

You meant I had to give up the world for my child, and now I want to give the world back to you. I would have like to know how it felt to give birth to a child of your grace and intelligence. I wish that you cherished your innocence.

Don't forget that I will not be far from your side always. Without forgetting that your eyes are mine as well, as I will forever look and see through your soul. Even when I perish, my energy will be felt around you—when you fall in love or give birth to your children. You are the bedrock of my religion and the base of my existence.

Xavier, my son, stands yourself up against the statues of great men; know that I, too, will use you as a measuring stick. You are my great son, a proud protégé of God! If something should ever happen to me, know that I will be with my Heavenly Father. Not everything you need to know about me is written in this book. I was, and am now, a mortal man who misses you more than I miss my own heart.

Since the day you children were taken from my side, I was not allowed to see you. I stayed strong, knowing that God's will is my motivation. We should be together someday. My heart in you makes the difference and is the determining factor in the courage of your days. Let your decisions be determined by the facts in all cases and let no one separate you from your heart. Remember to be a soldier of God. You must be with God so, stand as a Marine.

Now, Shelly, you shall be that missing piece of my heart that I might never find again. I shall cherish that relic and place it upon my chest, for you are my only purple heart in life. All my self-inflicted wounds aside, I want you to always look for the person closest to your heart; you'll find his eyes looking back at you. Because someone will love you more than your family does. Choose wisely.

Shelly, your wisdom is far superior to anything I have seen in any young lady. Your heart, your passion, your mercy becomes grace, and your wisdom will always outweigh your age. You are a blessed miracle of God. This world is a better place with you in it. I have seen far too many women run; you will succeed.

If you cannot see it, then it does not mean that it is not yours to keep. Faith is the strongest bond that connects us to God.

Be silent with your whispers, have hoped your eyes behold the glory of the Lord, and your emotions smell like light. From your heart, I see a flame when I look at you. You say I desire the whole world, and that is why God put you in it. For me, I need no explanation. I hold myself at the top of my intellectual abilities while waiting to read your mind.

To look through these dark tinted lenses will show me that the eyes of God, our Heavenly Father, sees life, although not as immaculate as Jesus Christ. Each bright beam of light, the brightest of rainbows, each splendid color being the beginning of a life force bound by God's Holy Spirit.

That binding light the presence of a multitude of souls, needs our Heavenly Father to see around hundred and eighty-degree angles from one end of the Universe to another. The Heavenly Father needs to see behind himself while looking forward through a vortex of time and space. We witness each beam of colorful light like a strand of DNA as an image of our incorruptible bodies.

My hope is that we will all join and bind together by God's Holy Spirit, traveling throughout the universe on one large beam of light. The solution that I propose may be able to curve this earth's gravitational direction.

Go with pride and answer your calling as you serve the Lord Jesus Christ. Be with God, not a wanderer. Lay not with the beast shall turn your tears into ashes, as we choke on the pollution of sinners.

I hope that with a watchful eye and a guiding light, the children's mightiest wings prepare their first freefall into the dreams of their fathers and mothers. The hardest duty to overcome is the horror that your eyes have seen, and the torture performed throughout our existence here on earth.

Don't you think that now is a time for healing? The blood will be the last thing He will remove from your hands, for you are worthy of the praise you gain by getting off your knees.

The one who is a great evangelist will visit you in good time. Be patient like our Heavenly Father, awaiting His descendants' return home. Experience says that your next steps should bring you closer to God; you will someday see Jesus Christ in the flesh.

I have not only seen Him, but I have also praised the feet that bore His weight and kissed the sandals He walks on. He was awed at my faith, my sight, and was absolute with His commands for His Angels.

In my life, I realized that I know nothing about fear and sin— disguised as pure hatred. I finally had a chance to reach out and ask for forgiveness for all my mistakes. This book is basically a eulogy.

We are all in God's presence, instituting a new way of life with different manners of speech, cultivating our thought. We will be the gathering of innocents empowered to create new destinations to bless this world with our brilliance.

If we fix nothing, then we have failed Him. Do your jobs. Let your boss know He is in charge. Provide Him with your projects. Let your mind stay focused. Close your mouth and let your heart forever be open. Will you say that some of the things are meant to last forever, and some things are not? Well, I am here to tell you everything can be recycled. When that time has expired, then the date is too late.

There will be adverse effects on our world if we don't act now. God gave me a gift that would not forbid you from experiencing the same kind of visions, and many do take part in that dream. I don't break promises. I try my best to keep them.

Cast your worries into the air. Throw my pages like confetti in front of your face. To laugh is to say that I am not the person that I say I am today. I am a father, a warrior, and a planner.

Let hatred not fill your heart with sadness. Overcome your grudges. Find your spirit, be fulfilled in Christ today.

People will understand that when you speak, either wisdom or ignorance will come from your mouth. Remember, ignorant people have nothing good to say. I don't live superior or inferior to others. Use your voice and be not afraid. Speak clearly and loudly enough to affect us all. Have you a great day and have a lovable existence? God blesses.

Part 2
Book of Prophecies

INTRODUCTION

M any legions of Angels have visited me over the course of my life. One Angel named Derdekea presented itself that moment in time as female. This Angel descended to earth for the salvation of humankind. Angels and humans consider her the supreme mother.

Derdekea sat with me for many days, telling me about the first battle in Heaven, how the Lord Jesus Christ's sacrifice saved the souls of His faithful followers. Born into a life of strange and unforeseen circumstances, this prodigal son has returned to serve a purpose through the Holy Spirit with the living will of God. I am blessed to have survived my strife.

I have had many messages delivered to me from benevolent celestial beings not seen by the common eye, only to be viewed by the gifted. My scripts are a testimony that shows me overcoming my adversities.

As Lucifer, the former Archangel, incarcerated us in sin at the time of Satan's deception of Adam and Eve, the masses of people were unaware that his rise to power is based upon our ignorance. However, the timeline to his redeemer assuming power is avoided by the evolution of humankind.

"So, that we may not be outsmarted by Satan. After all, we are not unaware of his intentions." (2 Cor 2:11 ISV) Bright beams of translucent light approached from out of Heaven. The wind began to blow, and voices were heard dancing in song. A brigade of Angels decided to visit me to play near a creek bed. I was a young man sitting on a hill, in the middle of a lush green pasture.

This was not the first-time Angels had visited me. It was important that I received messages from them. Enlisting the help of these Angels, I had begun placing images into words from visions received by their presence.

I had been a messenger of God most of my life, whispering with the Lord Jesus Christ, His Angels, and the twelve apostles with Saulos Tarseus in place of Judas. As I began to utilize my ability to understand the disposition of God, I transposed their messages as I wrote this manuscript.

In the height of the whispering between Jesus and His Angels of Light, He gave me many messages. The first message stated that there was once a time in Heaven when peace and prosperity reigned, the beginning designed for humans to inhabit the earth while worshiping Yahweh and Yeshua.

The last message was the theory for subatomic nuclear fusion; it is a geothermal, chilled water purifying, power generating apparatus. Jesus sent a select type of spirits to convey this message, like Nicola Tesla, Albert Einstein, Benjamin Franklin, Thomas Edison and many more.

As Satan battle against this Revelations Lucifer lost battle after battle, causing him to give up the war and control over my soul.

You are about to find out how a former Angel of Light called the Day Star turned against the will of our Heavenly Father.

"This does not surprise us. Even Satan changes himself to look like an Angel of Light." (2 Cor 11:14 NCV)

From that point on, Lucifer chose to become Satan to rule over the underworld and unleash his fury upon the unfaithful. Lucifer coerced many angels. Two-thirds of us Heavenly Father's Angels struggled to maintain the peace, while the opposing one-third battled and lost their positions in Heaven.

Lucifer knew not where his loyalties lay that day, as he was flung from his perch, hurled down to earth with his idiots. Satan thought that humans were malice with discontent, lazy, and undeserving.

The spirits of Our Heavenly Father Yahweh and his Almighty Son Yeshua, known as the Lord Jesus Christ, spent long hours resting with Adam and Eve until that morning. That is when the trouble began, and the story begins!

CHAPTER 1

An Angel's Message

Millions of lanterns burned brightly before the dawning of this God, before the Heavenly Father (Yahweh) created the laws of Moses, even before the existence of the Son of Man.

According to the written words of King Hezekiah, stated in the book of Isaiah 14:12-15 (KJV) [12] "How art thou fallen from heaven, O Lucifer, son of the morning! How art thou cut down to the ground, which didst weaken the nations! [13] For thou hast said in thine heart, I will ascend into heaven, I will exalt my throne above the stars of God: I will sit also upon the mount of the congregation, in the sides of the north: [14] I will ascend above the heights of the clouds; I will be like the most High. [15] Yet thou shalt be brought down to hell, to the sides of the pit."

Lucifer's throne was positioned above the stars in Heaven, directly above Yahweh's Kingdom. As the Heavenly Father conceived His son Yeshua who fell to earth and became Jesus Christ, Yahweh then created the Holy Spirit. Lucifer's first experience with the Holy Spirit split him into two as he began his deception.

Satan until this day denies the Holy Spirit. That is why he will be easily defeated.

Yeshua fought His father's battle inside the throne palace in Heaven. Lucifer staged a flirtatious affair with our Heavenly Father's most trusted and adored goddess, the mother of all beings. The Heavenly Mother named Holy Mary Mother of God, sat on the throne as the only one to carry the seeds that were to inhabit the earth after the union of souls commenced.

"And there appeared a great wonder in Heaven; a woman clothed with the sun and the moon under her feet and upon her head a crown of twelve stars." (Rev 12:1 NCV)

The arguments between Lucifer and his Anunnaki angels lasted exponentially over the course of millenniums; Satan was slowly persuading the other angels to join him. His army was fighting against the sovereign Lord inside the holy palisade. Evil was gaining control over the angels, whom most were fighting against the agreement between God and Man.

Recognize that the devil deceived Yahweh and the Holy Family into believing that His beloved goddess Mary was betraying Him by consorting with Lucifer. Now that Lucifer had the ability to split in to two because of the enormous powers given to him by Yahweh, he tried to capture the attention of the most trusted and adored goddess.

Lucifer crushed Yahweh's heart. Our Holy Mary Mother of God stands in awe. Lucifer had approached Mother Mary as she kept looking over Her shoulder, peering up the steps of the stadium, back up to the throne where our beloved Heavenly Father sat eating His wondrous baskets of fruits.

Enraged, His anger was aroused when His opposing angels tripped an alarm for war. The result would be the Immaculate Conception.

In anger, Yahweh sent bolts of lightning through the universe as the monumental presence of Yeshua declared war! The battle for Heaven was about to begin right there at Heaven's gate.

Satan licked the back of our Mother Mary's hand as an act of obsession. This act was uncommon for an Angel to perform such adornments toward God or His goddess in such a beloved manner.

The Heavenly Father sent His fury of lightning into the night's sky crossing the universe, causing the mantle to quake. From under this angel's flank, Satan spun Queen Mary around.

Lucifer's angels trapped Mother Mary; they began to drain the sack of seeds sewed within Her garment. Each seed was a soul planted in order to populate the earth.

As the lightning lit up the mantle of Heaven with bright flashes of atomic explosions that crackled across the vast darkness, the seeds landed on the floor of that galactic stadium. The souls were falling between the stone crevices of that coliseum, and the seeds spread out across the earth.

Heaven's gate was then broken as Satan gathered and devoured the souls that fell from this Goddess's purse. Satan grew in strength, charging through Heaven's gate, hell-bent on holy war!

The Holy Mary Mother of God was famished, as the life force of souls that were to inhabit the earth rained down upon the sands of Egypt, causing a civilization to flourish in a utopian garden, surrounded by God's Holy Spirit.

Satan had victory upon victory, as humans could not stand upright in the presence of evil. Now, however, we have the presence of the Lord Jesus Christ's supreme intellect to save us from the snares of Satan's wicked woes.

"So, rejoice you Heavens and all who live there! But it will be terrible for the earth and the sea because the devil has come down to you! He is filled with anger because he knows he does not have much time." (Rev 12:12 NIV)

The army of fallen angels that had surrounded our Holy Mary Mother of God started to anger the presence of Yeshua. Taking charge, the Trinity created a storm large enough that it scattered the rest of the seeds across the globe, enriching the earth with a passel of colors.

As the last seed fell into God's hands, it was one of the everlasting newborn stars to give light to their universe. He placed that seed tightly between His teeth, holding on, struggling not to drop that eternal star, Adonis.

Our Holy Mary Mother of God's purse was now emptied, all the souls that She was burdened to carry for our Heavenly Father, all the seeds are now scattered all over the vast wasteland.

While the presence of Yeshua contemplated His option to punish the fallen angels, His Father encompassed His Holy Spirit, the Trinity cohabitated within its presence still holding that eternal seed tightly between its clinched lips.

The Holy Mother Mary, who is the image of Mary Miriam's ultimate spiritual body was in a delicate condition bearing Her unborn child in Her womb. She did not want to let go of Her son (Yeshua), who will become Jesus and fall upon the sky on the Day of Judgment.

"This woman gave birth to a son who will rule all the nations with an iron rod. And her child was taken up to God and to His throne." (Rev 12:5 NCV)

Our Holy Mary Mother of God's sentencing, Her punishment, was carried out quickly, Yahweh sitting not on His throne, His anger outright, His palace at war, His goddess betrayed by Satan.

The Holy Mary Mother of God, a sworn keeper of the benevolent souls of the covenant, was now empty of souls. Delicate in Her pregnancy, She stumbled up the steps of that stadium, emotionally wounded, in much need of His love and protection. As She reached the entrance to the throne in the heights of that stadium, Yahweh threw Her from the palisade in a rage.

As Satan changed the outcome of Heaven and earth at that microscopic movement, Yahweh delayed Lucifer's punishments for accusing God of pandering with spirits.

The battle of principalities commenced when Lucifer began to mimic Yahweh's ultimate powers.

Satan's hatred for humanity was because he became the deceiver, praising, and adorning only himself. Lucifer became obsessed with Yahweh's absolute power. Lucifer the former Archangel was corrupt and jealous. This former General's lack of respect for Humankind all started with the betrayal of Yahweh too the deception of Adam and Eve.

"Then there was a war in Heaven. Michael and His Angels fought against the dragon, and the dragon and his angels fought back." (Rev 12:7 NCV)

Lucifer was stripped of his rank, and his right wing was ripped from his body. He deceived much of the fallen angels. The outcome and idea of an original agreement between God and Adam was a righteous purpose for the earth that eternally changed, when Satan failed, fell, and finalized his own eulogy.

Until then, we prepare the world for one of God's messengers, a prophet, an angel, a disciple of the Lord Jesus Christ. I have prayers protecting you, my readers. I have sent you messengers to cleanse your soul of all inequities, convey your prayers, count your atonements, bless the hands of the righteous, and hear the repentance of your soul through Jesus Christ, guided by God's Holy Spirit. You will see the truth through a unique set of eyes.

In the thrall of battle, Yahweh's anger subsequently pushed His queen, Mary the Mother of God, off the edge of His throne into the vat, entering a black hole from where there was no return. She was immortal within the halls of the palisade; thrown from the palace gate She was now destined to become a mortal being subject to death. Mary the Mother of God travelled through these dominions of time. By the time She made Her travel to the earth's surface, She had entered the realm of the Israelites in a day of matrimony, a union between bride and groom.

Landing and tumbling down this mountain, Her body was scarred and beaten upon the rocks of this coarse terrain. As She landed face down in the mountain region, She fell into the palms of Mary. Both Mary and Yeshua were aided by the Holy Spirit, both spirits of our Holy Mary Mother of God and Yeshua's spiritual anomalies, their souls entered Mary Miriam's body, resulting in Her pregnancy.

The Holy Spirit then helped her to her fleet. Placing her on solid flocks of Angels, Yahweh then noticed that she was pregnant with child. The Immaculate Conception was the decision of Yeshua's choosing Mary Miriam for her spiritual wealth and eternal knowledge. Mary the Virgin Mother of God was virtually sinless, as holy as can be.

To keep Mary from being stoned, He then placed Mary upon a path, led by God's Holy Spirit. God's conception had occurred. The baby Jesus lay silent within her womb. She sought Joseph to lay her burden upon him as the war raged on in Heaven.

Yahweh, dressed as a Roman centurion mounted His horse, returning to Rome to report as Caesar. Yahweh was off His throne, now sitting upon a horse in front of Mary Miriam. Caesar was the ruler of the entire world; the Trinity surrounded Him; allowing His will to be done. The child must be born, grow wise, fulfilling the prophecies to be our savior, sacrificed for the sins of the world, rise, and ascend upon His throne in Heaven.

Caesar or Yahweh knew He must sacrifice Yeshua for Jesus to be King. So, by the time Jesus was born, Caesar attempted to kill all first-born sons in the land, but Mary and Joseph hid, until Jesus became strong in the Word of God. Yahweh knew not how to stop Jesus' crucifixion. Jesus Christ sacrificed His life to teach about love and honor. Before His execution, He preached about peace.

The Lord Jesus Christ's body was torn; His blood ran down the step in the throne in Rome. Christ's ancestors already grown and roaming the land. The descendants of David's bloodline stretched far beyond the wall, Jerusalem, or Israel. Caesar was not aware of the sacrifice made for the world that day.

Our beloved Michael, the Archangel, filled with the Holy Spirit, then broke the right wing of the angel now known as Satan. Michael banished Satan and his Anunnaki angels from out of the palisades, never again to return within the palace wall. The fallen angels scoured the earth, searching for victims to manipulate. The celestial bodies not viewed by the common eye, only viewed by the gifted and the blessed.

I don't just see Satan, I know when he arrives because of his hatred his light isn't as bright as Heavenly Angels, his smell is as wretched as a thousand dead horses, and he is cursed. While reading his mind, because of Lucifer's weaknesses I can hear what he is thinking and desires most. In the constant devouring of souls, the angels of darkness have only thirst and their love for destruction while serving their dark lord, Lucifer.

"The great dragon was cast out, that serpent of old, called the Devil and Satan, who deceives the whole world; he was cast to the earth, and His Angels were cast out with him." (Rev 12:9 KJV)

Only a supreme being can take down the Antichrist; can only be brought down by the grace and glory of the Lord. The only thing that lays this immortal being in his grave permanently is the words of God Himself from the mouth of the Lord Jesus Christ.

The Antichrist will be convicted when the Lord Jesus Christ vocally synchronizes His subsonic electromagnetic pulsating voice that sacrifices, by crushing the spirit and the souls the Antichrist collected.

The Antichrist made a final attempt to cast lots and place wages of how prophetic I was, because of the benevolent choral of my King.

As far back as I can see, I remember the walk with my King, the Lord Jesus Christ. I become one of many brothers of the Lord Jesus Christ. I don't deny him.

With Christ's body on the cross, He turned and saved the world with his selfless act of love and kindness. Eternally grateful with much sorrow, I will not decline my call to battle and shall never forget Him.

Show no fear, you are God's warriors, meant to serve and prevail as part of our Heavenly Father's legion of Angels. Each day we fight Satan's curse: sin. Battling close to the frontline of God's army has led to the privileged knowledge and overpowering wisdom that His love might save me someday.

I am here to serve and protect my brother's decree:

To fight for those who are far too weak, and to defend the meek against the reign of evil men that left a path from Heaven broken with destruction. Satan left his misery at every doorstep, including the persecution of Christians for our belief in Christ our Lord. He died for us all that day.

God has recognized my ancestors, who were separated from each other for many years. Our greatest memory was the fall of our walls in Germany. Guarded in our hearts forever, my ancestors sacrificed themselves for the Lord Our Savior, Jesus Christ.

In my father's land, my ancestors were represented by a knighthood belonging to the Templar Knights, for our braveries in the Holy Crusades. Who stood before the Freemasons in Jerusalem sometime in the eleventh century?

This added to the legend, the essence of my family's origin that resides deep within my soul. Deep within God's soul, forever scrolled upon His heart, buried, and born again in His name.

I was about to come into the world alone and scared. It seemed as if I was defenseless, left without any protection except for God's gracious gift of sight, filling my mind with visions and the ability to see past life into the realm of the dead.

The starlight that burned brightly is the illumination of my Father's saber. The reflection of His eyes radiates with the love He has shared with me. They are my descendants, the last of my family's seeds cast between the sea and sand. We are living in the times when we the people begin to rebuild our republic, participance of a lost belief that happens to be a cross between Judaism and Christianity.

I have always answered my call of duty whenever Christ called upon me to perform divine acts of kindness. Blessed to have survived, to have experienced and recorded the events I have been blessed enough to witness.

I have always been in it for a new adventure, a journey that glorifies God. I help untangle the web of deceit that Satan spat from his lips, trying to lure me away from God's presence.

His lies are far too weak to call upon to battle his bird of prey. Satan waited until my life was in ruins before unleashing his griffin upon me, grinding my bones into dust, cutting into my flesh, piercing my skin, placing it like an old Ferret coat upon his skeleton.

That monster sought to take my life at an early age. Yet, I was destined to be a writer; here is my storytelling what makes me a Son of God.

The pestilence that plagued my father was alcoholism, an abnormality known to be genetic, it never took with me. My father assisted in the precipitation the reign of my adolescent dreams now to become your reality.

When I was born, the church bell struck, and the Angels sang to the sounds of those Heavenly Trumpets, showing the signs that the beginning of a new day, an everlasting era, was soon at hand.

The end has yet to come. I was numbered and counted, written in the constellations forever to fight forces only seen through the Holy Spirit. I am bound by honor as an overseer of the meek. I am battling forces not seen by the eye of mortal men, but to be that presence surviving by God's Grace. My wish is to become our Heavenly Father's supreme Angel.

I am sworn to uphold the code of the life—life being the second rule and the first being love. I am to learn from mortal men to bend and flex as if a reed was my destiny, learning about higher powers not taught at Yale or in any book at Harvard.

I was premature, blinded by the sight of sin, the fact of life, born of a cocaine-drip nose job and the ruins of a wicked marriage. Left alone, this youngling was in eminent danger. Every time I was left alone; I always came close to death.

CHAPTER 2

From the Outside Looking in

I was receiving messages directly from Heaven. I was witnessing many epiphanies during a dark time in the creation of this world. I was strong, confident, and intellectually brilliant.

These spiritual revelations had been knocking on my door since I was a small child. I know many Angels who have told me of miracles that they have performed in their duties for God.

It was God's intention for me to obtain the ability to look beyond life into the eyes of death to see the horizons that God intended all his followers to believe. Of course, with the proper medication, I could control my thoughts while ignoring the sights of ghostly arrivals.

As sure as I lay there on that table in that medical clinic, I surely was my brother's keeper. I see each vision like daydreams, causing personality flaws in my character. People think because I see and hear the dead that I must be crazy.

To see godliness in my neighbor's eyes, as my eyes well up with tears for the passionate premise. Our backs against the wall with humanity raging war opposed the principles of Christ Jesus that said love and prayer bound us together through the Holy Spirit. Truly God blesses believers who have built their faith through their years of service, bound by the light of Jesus Christ.

Even when God's Holy Spirit presents itself to me, He is one of the strongest presences I have ever witnessed. His beauty surpasses any splendor this world should offer.

The visual reality is far beyond my wildest dreams, and his love is endless. The Trinity gives a child command over a gift for that young child to control. When that gift becomes a burden, his yoke becomes too much weight as he bows his head to pray.

I have had far more activity with Heavenly beings in the last few years more than I like to talk about. Multitudes of Angels have graced me with their presence, all of them giving warning that global dominance is completely under our control.

Chosen or left behind to witness, I am comforted by thoughts of our Lord Jesus never leaving our side. I anticipate fellowshipping on the day Jesus' eyes peer into my own. I know I will be part of a legion of Angels on the day of my resurrection.

The fall of two brothers is what Nostradamus predicted, and 2012 was the beginning of Satan's reign in other parts of this galaxy, places he was unable to find until our sun shone, and the planets aligned with the center of the Universe. Later an Antichrist disguised as a great mediator will rise, and this world will be at an end.

The next step in my journey was to exit the hospital, reentering the jungles of Saint Petersburg. When my eyes opened, I was three days in a psychiatric hospital. My sight was now able to view the benevolent celestial beings, as well as the paranormal.

I was complaining of unfortunate family interference. They were pumping plenty of good food in me as I regained my mental health.

A dense dark fog had appeared out of nowhere. The morning was gloomy with shadows lurking in the mist. I could see the brightness of the sun piercing through the fog, not bright enough to break through the boundaries of this mental prison. I stood outside peering through this haze of what was an opening of a very clear window, scouting the fence line, contemplating an escape.

A door then opened. A Chinese American warrior walked up behind me. He was one of the first spirits I remember speaking to after my near drowning. He walked out from Heaven's gate.

I idolized this warrior; it was Master Bruce Lee in his ultimate spiritual presence angelic in every way. He placed his hand upon my shoulder. I could feel the energy from his penumbra. I could see him with my peripheral vision.

He said to me, "If you think that fall is worth breaking both our necks, don't think. How about trying a subtler approach?" His body was not of this world. His spirit was a part of the sun's illumination that penetrated the fog that early morning hour.

Bruce's presence had been in many battles. A master of his arts, he was a spiritual warrior traveling the galaxy after his death, fighting battles for the Heavenly Father.

It was not until I told him how to build lights that saber that the odds shifted in his favor. He appeared to be a part of radiant light beaming off the aura of his presence. I was receiving messages from Heaven about this technology, and he was eager to obtain the knowledge I had about thermodynamics.

The process of subatomic nuclear fusion is partly that of a device that can propel a beam of light beyond the boundaries of on ordinary weapon. It can repel and deflect a trajectory of bullets and bring together a field of force that allows soldiers to go unharmed.

Although I was drowsy from the medication, I saw many things that made sense inside my visions. The legion of Angels that I had witnessed so many times received. God's blessings because of time spent with these warriors of God as Angels of Light.

God's commands implemented, as His Angels told me tales of epic battles with Satan and his army of angels. How the devil was clever and cunning, having such a powerful effect over most matters in this universe. He was like a fox in a henhouse, sacrificing us humans like chickens.

You don't have to see him to know he is there, and if you did not feel his presence, then you might be turning a blind eye as you head straight toward a catastrophe. Of course, faith is our defense against the fear that he brings.

Along with the whispers of God's Heavenly Angels, many people who have died have succumbed to my abilities. They are willing participants. I could prophesize an end to their spiritual agony, help their passions, while easing a bit of their pain. Either by answering a question, sending a message to an Archangel, or simply praying for God's Holy Spirit to intervene.

Many more of the disembodied spirits are restless, sleeping with the damned, because they have not enough knowledge to pray to God to light their path after their physical death. The spirits need guidance because of their suffering due to their spiritual incarceration in Hades. Shame keeps them from entering through Heaven's gate. Those spirits would rather sit in a bed of thorns than ask for redemption.

It was a tour of duty in many ways. I was always visited by many circles of spirits who were on a quest for scriptural or visionary insight into their spiritual incarceration.

I was using prayers to control these spirits' destination by harvesting the power of my holy temple, my ultimate spiritual being. I found an ability to fulfill my innate purpose, indeed, to speak and converse with the lost forms of energy, which are living outside God's grace.

As a human and an angel of God, we help them see the light—people who have committed accidental suicide or ones who have died to suddenly and refuse to follow His light.

The oracle that was a gifted presence, not forgetful of who she is and where she is from, or how she got there, was of course the light of my grandmother. It was difficult for me. I always felt her presence.

Colors of her aura, the light of her soul that made it possible for me to see her. I cried for many days as I witnessed her beauty. It had been eighteen years since I had seen her. I thought I was going mad with these hallucinations strapped to that hospital bed.

I was no longer upset with God. He gave my grandmother back to me as a guide. I learned more about why God blessed me with this gift. It might have something to do with my near drowning or failed attempts at suicide. It brought Satan close again, trying to confuse me to corrupt my resolve.

It is very upsetting to me to witness things that others think are mere hallucinations. I hear ghosts' voices as a delayed reaction to their movements, lights that pierce my eyelids and wake me from a sound sleep, or other loved ones delighting my dreams.

I further converse with souls with such power that my grandmother beams her light upon every subject. I had the honor and privilege of persuading important people who could otherwise be manipulated by Satan's powers. I have seen as many evil spirits as I have comforted good ones. Many lost souls would ask God to reveal a purpose in their spiritual being, asking for the ability to travel to different dominions.

I was acting as a ticket taker while praying for guidance, directing any spirit out of harm's way, into God's hands or His awaiting Angels. I would be a comfort to many who had lost their way. Their circumstances caused those difficulties, making them unable to figure out for themselves how to pass through to another dimension.

Figuratively speaking, if the Heavenly Father is in the eighth dimension, and we live in the third dimension, then the embodied are between the fourth and fifth dimensions. If you make it past the sixth dimension, you shall pass panels of judges in the seventh, and by the time you have made it to the eighth, our universe will look like a flat pane of stained glass, and all that bleeds between it has arose.

The stars stand complacent upon His crown as the Lord Jesus Christ rebukes Satan's pontifications of his army. Jesus' dynamic soul-crushing cosmic vocals place Him in a reflection of perfection.

Jesus stands before a multitude of Angels, those brave bringers of peace, I stood beside with Him, waiting for Him to enlighten me with more visions because securing divine wisdom with His knowledge helps us perform our duties. Scripture is the base; the bible is the key. I was taught from an earlier age when my grandmother instructed me how to decipher codes within the bible. God has His fingerprints on every printed page.

CHAPTER 3

The Awakening

Trust in no one, for it is a vicious world, and you shall surely seek deceit. Attack and you shall move yourself further into defeat. Withdraw, and men will call you a coward. Stumble and they will call you weak. Be braggadocios, and you may be known as boastful. However, when you whisper while speaking the truth, men shall call you meek.

I know that my ex-mother-in-law, Roberta's body shall be devoured by cancer from the smoke that hovered around her tomb while she used her own Angel as prey. She was worse than any hyena. Worms will forever eat at her flesh while maggots tear apart her chest, exposing her turret heart used only as an instrument of war.

After my outpost of water recedes below my bow, the breakers are far too many, as I drown my troubles deep into the ocean blue. Savannah is my haven, my guiding light. She brings me comfort. The burdens of my life are the duality of mothers.

I always felt I had to choose one mother or the other. As if I could not have, both love me. I accused Savannah of battling a storm much greater than her, sworn to control our heart's emotions the reality of these cages of fear of an eternity in hell, this mental abnormality living within me.

My vessel was bound on a course that only God had control over. Roberta corrupted the cistern of where we need to drink.

Savannah was my companion when I was her steed. I was worthy of her love when she gave it, fetching for her affections when it was every pupil's dream to have an oracle as one's teacher.

God handed Savannah two cherry red apples to stow for her success in raising her fine young lads. As those young apples grow to full maturity, they flourish as healthy, respectable people, making their way through life, spindling the cocoon from a flower, sprouting wings.

Savannah was generous enough to take me and my brother under her wing when our mother had decided to live in another part of the state with her boyfriend. Savannah comforted me when I was thirteen and alone in the world. She deserved those apples to stow.

Angelically our Heavenly Father is known to appear as the Monarch. Serendipitously, we stand in His garden, as we begin to grow in wonderment, flying is one of our many strengths. As we glide throughout the backyards of these gardens, shaking the leaves of the apple trees. High into the trees, under an orchard of apples, we land, waiting for that precious Angel who could not resist such an awesome bloom.

It was our duty to guard its flourishing nectar, never to devour, bend that branch, allowing the life to flourish, drawing the nutrients from underneath her roots. Our tree was not to be eaten, cherished blessings from above not to be consumed, polished in that ray of sunlight.

The monarch's cider is dripping down each corner of that erect building of boxes. He says His prayers by the harvest. To hold a spear in His right hand is to give good label to our crispy green apples, the saplings have yet to turn red, something that our Heavenly Father's eyes may never have to see again. Before He gives up the cider business, you can find Him adjusting His bifocals with a glass of wine in His hand.

Bridges are built in this manner. Cabins will splinter, while mountains shall crumble to His feet. The monarch awaits His sons, kneeling before their Heavenly Father. We are then commended to the fields to defend His foes.

We become litigators for our Heavenly Father, the monarch of our family. We justify forgiving God's enemies.

We overcome adversities by praying for your opponent's souls.

As the monarch seemly awaits the passing of holidays, as the harvest may begin another year and yet an abundance of fortunes, bring good soil under mother's feet and chopsticks in all the children's hands, the children act as if the sticks are swords battling with the other brothers and sisters with great might and nobility.

These saplings are now on the run, with smiles upon their faces, with apples stuck between their teeth, chasing down Mother with her gardening buggy. She was planting a rose garden while the young men and young women place orchids in their mother's hair, as our Heavenly Father observes, knowing that she is the apple of His eye.

I was nothing other than a puppet to my Heavenly Father, this master of men with many disguises. We were His finely tuned piano band. This performing pianist, entertaining his Heavenly Father's company in the living room, filled with His gentle friends.

The friends and family gather to harvest His apples. They were ready to fire up the urns, to bake stalks of hay when the apples refuse to freeze with the rivers of mysterious climate change frosting the families' orchard that year.

Even as Roberta got her second chances, she failed to perform God's ordainments. He has no sympathy for fools who seldom bow before a God to pray.

As the song (Call Me When You're Sober, by: Evanescence,) "You cannot play the victim this time." The poetry assisted in my heart was for Luna (Amy Lee) to experience many moons under the ridges of my tongue.

We stood not for the freedom of our minds, yet at the mercy of God, failing to cast drugs aside, the sigh of relief that kept marijuana not far from us.

In the practices of lies, these practical witches show us that love costs more than honey. As much care as it takes to cultivate that hive, you think the bees were giving it away for free. Marvelous drones harvest your sweet nectar filling your heart and mind with words.

I am turning your thoughts into emotions. You must be busy bees to churn that sweet nectar of a honeycomb, pounds of pollen infesting their queen's lair. As the workers brave the heat, your palace is pristine your love is à la carte.

We all lack in faith some time or another, although the path we choose will bridge our gaps. As we reached the halfway point in releasing our spirit to God, the stronger the devil dared to push us back. Satan is a hard bird to tackle, far worse angel to tame, the cost of this is through his lack of salvation and the number of souls he is willing to cage.

God is steadfast, fighting for us every moment of His day. We must be willing to stand up for the Lord Jesus Christ. I see how much He sacrifices for us. Each moment of His breath is one last precious gift to us. Jesus hopes that His people will join and believe.

Each person that stands on the outside of God's wall, His heart, or His mind, is one more victim. We must sacrifice ourselves until He chooses to devote His blessings to us bathing in His beauty and splendor.

As our bodies are stripped to bare bones, draining our sheets, I was drowning in a sea of broken bones. My clothes, this computer, a few scrap sheets of papers, describe the insurmountable pain, my agony of rebirth. Waking up from this mental abnormality was like exiting a clear pool with nothing on, feeling the freedom of vanity dripping off my limbering body parts.

I woke up from one of my first dreams in many years. I could hear my offspring playing in the living room. The excitement was in their voices, making my heart cry out in desperation despite the differences I was having in my mind at the time. I was experiencing a lot of swelling within my heart. I was waking from a bliss-filled sleep, pretending that reality was a bad dream and my life just another nightmare.

Waiting at the water's edge, serenely, sincerely, subsequently, I laid down my head face first in a coma, waiting to place myself under without any breath within my lungs to exhale. We were to become slayers of unimaginable feats behind these allegations.

There was no lewd act made, except burning our ships on the shores of the Jordan River that vessel shall remain clean like shimmers of light inside my sights for these lies to become my illusion.

The story went from my drowning to my cover up, where I thought if I lied about the sin that brought my marriage into ruins then you would forgive me for that sin. I realized that it had to be the truth told for any forgiveness to take place.

I felt good, as though God was setting trials before me, leading me to a greater yield in life. When I was called upon to battle, it is in my heart and my mind that God's will change the circumstances of my unfortunate proceedings. Causing a revolutionary turn of events with magnificent outcomes that will set my soul free.

Taking my rightful place beside my queen called to arms and is ready to battle. All you must do when in danger is lay hands upon your opponent and walk through them. The harvesters nurture those sweet supple apples when the time comes; indeed, they are prepared for anything.

Each apple symbolizes a person connected to a stock of that same root and nutrients, burrowed in the same soil. We end up with a plantation of food that never spoils, accounting for every apple each year the harvest enters and begins another generation.

In my dream, a silhouette of Pocahontas was smoking a peace pipe in the living room. I snapped out of this dream, eyes wide open, and mouth tightly shut. It took years before Josephine traded me off for something sleek.

I am not the kind of person to give unnecessary corrections or apologies for Josephine's actions that is something as poetic as walking down a cloister, to bow to her tenders. In her mercy, her strength was her credential. If my potential is to curl the lips of that benevolent church, her beauty is like boundaries of harvesters howling throughout the trees.

The meaning of my life with Josephine was like strolling down a flower-filled garden with different pleasant-smelling passionflowers overhead. In that moment, we forgot why we hated each other so much, and when we kissed again love surrounded us and Jesus was there witnessing our union.

The falling of the branches in our orchard of apple influences the earth's soil enriching the dirt beneath His feet as the air, we breathe, He sees. I shall not falter, kneeling at the founder of the fountain of everlasting life and love.

The reliable Heavenly Father breathes like streams of steam billowing from His frostbitten lips, chalices within His hands. He shall stimulate your nurturing nature, tips of His togs buttoning down the front of His overcoat, drinking from the tops of His tears, breathless, without speech beneath His rolling lips. Thunder plays between His ears. He is the status erectus. He is my dire need of life. Heaven in its divine exquisiteness sure sounds nice.

The battle began when our God became a Father and sent His Son to save us from our sins. To stand in the shadow of that all-knowing God, I knew that it was only a matter of time before my criminal charges were gone.

It changed my ways of thinking, making it pleasurable to obtain the deep satisfaction of helping these hindered spirits free, the forces that lay crosses at my feet, securing His sworn cherishment to proceed in the accordance of light He has provided for me.

In the beginning, when God created man and woman, He cherished these righteous people while embracing the blessings that He gifted. He took pity on the poor, while He honored the meek. We should seize the priority, the ultimate purpose of every Christian man, woman, or child. That prayer is our microphone to God, and insight or foresight is a blessing to have before you need the information.

The youngsters were full of joy, excited to be with me. To see me smile, although I had an expression of fear plain as daylight upon my face, the tension was in my voice. These children knew that something had gone wrong, and their father was struggling with his faith.

The expressions on my children's face explained that their inexperience with a deceitful parent their mother ponders of thoughts revenge. The children's facial features sadden my soul that as your father I was exiled from your existence.

Josephine's depression setting in the punch bowl filled with a plethora of fine-tasting marijuana, relentlessly getting high. On and in a constant deflowering, twice nightly this was a regular delight. It was a frequent, daily family recurrence of drug abuse almost every night.

Our sheets were torn, tattered, worthless regards of garbage. I had been placed in troubled times, clinging to my need to mend my ways. The blessings were upon my back. God's spirit surrounded me.

I was searching for the truth. I searched for God yet refused to turn to God to receive the glory of His blessings. For the Lord is my shepherd I shall not want, yet I fear not returning to His flock from out of the darkness. I was leading them with the answers to life's mysteries to reveal a new prospective behind the Holy Ghost.

As a person, I can see through the mask that people parade around wearing. To see the reason why people, place those masks upon their faces in the first place, disguising their fears, that prelude to jealousy that builds upon anger that leads to defeat.

In all God's beauty, his descendants must learn to communicate with the Lord Jesus Christ's principals, penances, properly articulating communications with Him. It will help them in their future as they become adults.

It is important to instruct them from the moment you meet, leaving them with your gifts of wisdom and insight. God's blessings will return to you. Your actions will have results, multiplied in the massive amounts of energy through the presence of the Almighty, the Lord Jesus Christ.

Fight through. Be prepared, knowing the ransoms the Antichrist is willing to demand. Life continuously spirals toward creating Heaven more like earth. A second war will rage in Heaven when Satan and his misfits' angels attempt to escape from hell. The Lord Jesus Christ calls upon all Heavenly Angels to defend the towers to preserve our existence and the new foundation in Heaven.

Like Albert Einstein said, "Energy cannot be created nor destroyed." Surely, Satan was caged for an eternity. When that time arrives, he will have forgotten his name and caught without guard. Jesus Christ has the knowledge that once we adjourn together in Heaven, we will have an intellectual ability to sense the presence of wickedness.

If living in sin has turned you against the will of God, make your path right before Satan casts further doubts upon your soul. Focus your sight on the target, release all your raw emotions, and make your mark with love. Let your lips be loose, allow your words to come freely and openly, let your heart be an open book for all to read.

If your mind is penetrated with thoughts of confusion, change the subject; you are glorified in the eyes of the Lord. Ask and you shall receive. Speech sows like seeds. He shalt when listening. Seek, and sight be given. Taking part in Christianity is by finding and praising the ones you love and praying for the ones who oppose you.

Let the Lord Jesus Christ's provisions illuminate the direction of your path. Clear your heart of fear. Have strength. Ask for redemption, while having your sins forgiven because of your prayers or that blessing will not deserve our Heavenly Father's approval.

Keep being persistent. He will notice your progress, creating a utopia, an environment of perfection, if you believe in the Lord Jesus Christ. He Himself needs your prayers in this ongoing struggle, this seemingly endless battle over countable souls.

God's Heavenly Angels appear with forewarnings falling in place before actions can evolve. I will see a shining object in the middle of darkness pinpointing the Angel's direct incoming path and indirect exit strategy.

Those Angels of God are always suited with armor and have some form of weaponry on them that distinguishes them from others. No angel is greater than others are, unless you are an Archangel. They are the guardians and have sovereignty over the majority in Heaven. The service they perform for our Heavenly family is without a question to the point and procedure magnanimous.

When spirits come into my vicinity, my guardian angel always greets them. Stating a purpose to their visit, they are determined safe or hostile. My guardian angel is always there, and my grandmother is never far away.

I have received theories of subatomic nuclear fusion from some of the great minds of our time: Albert Einstein, Nikola Tesla, Benjamin Franklin, Thomas Edison, etc. They have filled my mind with amazing achievements. The enigmatic language used to communicate the data to me is brought to us in the form of white noise in use of telepathy.

Angels and spirits live around every person and are preyed upon if you are not living in the Word of God. Your actions cause a chain reaction on a paranormal plateau.

If all that is in your heart is anger, fear, jealousy, or hatred. Then, the Angel of Light leaves and dark angels come to collect your soul.

Surround yourself with the Holy Spirit; always cleanse yourself of all inequities so you may be in the presence of the Almighty Son, so your prayers will be answered. This cleanses your soul, so the Lord Jesus can communicate for you to our Heavenly Father.

Angels of Light get injured superficially; of course, the most effective wound happens to be their pride. The thought of losing a soul or failing at a task is a constant emotion that plagues the Angels. It is free will that surrenders the human over to Satan and his fallen angels.

The Angel of Light battles to preserve righteousness, but Satan has a number in mind, and he wants to store all the worst to fight the Lord in Heaven once more. That battle will happen after humankind has been extinct for many years.

That is why we as Christians are responsible of collecting souls, cleansing sin through baptism, providing hope that salvation is closer than we think.

CHAPTER 4

Without Boundaries

There was one awaking vision that I could remember. I believed the government's satellites would soon be visiting, us watching over us from outer space. It was nearing the year of 2016, now we are here to believe change is good. Start this process by teaching the children new government policies with a one-union Republic. It will improve our way of life. It is a part of humanity evolving.

The government has several channels on the monitor, calculating certain probabilities about the population's growth, agricultural interest, sexual reproduction, and of course quality of life.

Some agents found the satellites to be a breach in our freedom to have privacy. We were monitored by one of the first satellites watching over specific progenies of interest. These satellites were in place sometime in the earlier eighties when President Reagan first learned about us, by then he subsequently forgot our names.

It was not until the Clinton administration when the awareness of this lost project was brought about that made this power program that more interesting in the development of human behavior.

The diplomats watched while waiting, they saw everything while listening to conversations without warrant. I later found out this was a superstition, the product of a disorder.

When I believed, I had a supreme mind, the thoughts of the government spying upon us was a prelude of acts to come. We have witnessed great signs that soon many will witness the fall of a great nation into the hands of the Jesus Christ!

That night's vision was medically induced about what would befall this nation in the years to come, the evil that will take control over this once devoted nation of God.

Until our government casts many sinister people who now crowd the halls of congress, diplomats that have overstayed their term. They are attempting to turn this Republic into a Communistic regime, a socialist party.

Politicians loathing, greedy, worshiping money over God, betraying humanity, stealing, murdering while raping the people's children of this great society. We are allowing large corporations and politicians to continue embezzling money for the rich while strangling the poor.

There will be a day when no law will hold them accountable for their actions. They will have complete anonymity, for the minority of the people will be stepped upon, casting their bodies in a field, watching them burn as that soulless corporation collects its tickets as it sucks the life out of our planet.

These large corporations will turn to the sky to spy with satellites, hearing behind closed doors. These tools will bring about much chaos for they will control the currents of the winds and tides of the sea.

Like the night, this woman brought her spirit into our homes. Dressed in a black designer suit, calling a dark ceremony, in this vision she used one of the government satellites to peer into the privacy of dwellings.

Hell, cometh was a Politian and a student of witchcraft. Like Roberta, Hell, cometh was a murderous heathen with a plan to raise the dead. She executed evil deeds, worshiping her own acts of indiscretions.

With evil intent, Hell, cometh was using innocent souls, the purity of prophetic youths, on a noble bloodline from Germany. She had to pull into the house four female spirits that sat among us.

Hell, cometh attempted to remove information by playing some sort of card game, foretelling fortunes to predict her future. She was a spiritual master in witchcraft. The Antichrist was the dead they needed to rise, and the Presidency was the power she needed to reign supreme.

This woman was alone, not standing with any counsel. These quests played out with the utmost need for desecration to utter her secrets. To have her involved in such practices proves that she was not the devoted Protestant that she proclaimed to be.

The images that I saw of her were, for the most part, the outline of her character. This woman was on the search for information that led her to a sacred book that had no place in a political office. The Egyptian books of the Dead the ancient manual.

Witnessing many things during this spiritual cyanosis, I could see for the most part her outline among the shadows while the spirits conversation was continuous. Most of the manner of speech, in tongues or plain body language, suggest that evil was afoot. I was tending to the children while paying no mind to the woman behind the stainless flask.

I noticed that for some reason, I felt like I was used for some sort of political and spiritual propaganda. This woman's heart being as dark as her intelligence, Hell, cometh was deeply saddened with the courses of ugly men in her life. She was scorned from the beginning, yet she picked the used and useless ones to perform her dirty deeds (counterintelligence, cover-ups, and murder).

Why did she somehow witness my channel, other than circumstances pertaining to my gift to converse with the spirits, or battles of the damned and demonic? I was having the chance to witness the Lord Jesus Christ firsthand. Hell, cometh was interested in my near-death experiences and my resurrections of life (my children). This woman knew that there was something secretive about my circumstances, something to do with my revelations supported by scripture.

Hell, cometh, needed to use my world as a porthole to gather some much-needed explanation to spells left binding in turmoil. These four spirits are resting in peace with one another, sent to uncover an old tale by a fallen patriarch.

Looking around I could see that the four spirits that surrounded this table of cards were four states of mind not alive in the presence of my children.

The first spirit that got my attention was the one that I must have spent many moments with. I was looking around to see if my grandmother could be visible. Out of sight, yet within my mind she whispered, "I'm still here."

However, these women must have been close in some relation to God. I am sure that they obtained the ability to read one's mind, receiving the spiritual gift of intuition. Everyone except, the mortal woman digging for bones in my flower patch was aware that telepathy was truly a seventh sense in nature.

The essence of nature that draw these goddesses to occupy reflections of light beaming off the aura of their souls, they had the ability of telepathy, their objectives will be made clear later tonight.

All I was to do was to watch the game of cards as each face fell befriending their fortunes. Perceiving Hell, cometh messages were secret something to do with the rebirth of a spirit. Bar Jesús were once a sorcerer and false prophet. (Acts 13:6) "⁶And when they had gone through the isle unto Paphos, they found a certain sorcerer, a false prophet, a Jew, whose name was Barjesus:" In this world now a Wiccan warlord sent back to destroy the earth.

Bar Jesús was the name given by an angel sent to become the superior antichrist. Bar Jesús was a man that lived during the crucifixion of Jesus a concept of evil's power disguised in this universe and personal friends of Caiaphas. Satan's descendants his sons, Bar Jesús with his false prophet, they are no Angels. He is believed to be a male born once before, most loved by his peers, blinding us with booty, paralyzing us with words of fear and ungodliness.

The most current name of the antichrist is Bar Jesús Caduceus means "He has been persuaded by a former rogue angel that presented him with a Herms staff as his symbol of his power. With two serpents entwined and climbing vertically on the staff surmounted by two Angel wings."

It was my observation that this woman, Hell, cometh was helping the Antichrist rise before his time. She was his servant in the true fashion of her manner. She was visiting him in his presence, the preferences of maliciousness, her character flawed. I am having several visions of this woman. I had found out that she only served her own purposes— greed, power, murder, vanity, and corruption.

Filled with the power of insight, this intellectual woman could bring about action, causing result in a spiritual world to know she was in contempt. She used the Word of God to spit taunts back into His face. She had the strongest of wills among the spirits that night.

She was bound to this wicked game of cards that had unfolded in my presence, as the juveniles and I were enjoying the evening. The spirits did not move from place to place; they stayed stationary. The mortal woman moved her device about the world, roaming from boom to doom, freely taking notes, placing wagers, and gathering debts.

This woman was aware of my troubles. She knew about the criminal charges and my arrests, even the medications I was taking. She was seeking the placement of a mystical book of spells. Prayers that not only exonerate her deeds, but entice her will, giving into her passions, to resurrect a presence known only as Bar Jesús Elías Caduceus now his current name will be Ramon Cade tress. To show the world, so we will witness his supremacy.

There was no saving this woman from the wrongs that she had acquired over the years of lying in public office. She was willing to sacrifice herself with many others to reign superior in not only this world, throughout the galaxy. This woman has everything to do with the rising of this superior being known as the Antichrist.

I can only call this woman by the codename Hell, cometh. Presently, Hell, cometh plays with her frizzy hair. I was watching the cards while my younglings carry a flush over this pilot in control of her device (satellite). She was observing many families far in outer space. These actions not out of the realm of possibility. Not made clear in this world of spiritual chanting, I longed for some explanations behind this ghostly visitation.

She was seeking to destroy anyone who stood in her way. The quest was for herself to be an all-knowing superior being. She lives and will forever live with wickedness in her heart because she is evil. All the knowledge in the world will serve only one purpose, to sustain herself with religious references.

She completely misunderstood and underestimated me as a messenger of our Heavenly Father. God's will be served that night, as I was an able observer of that candlelit festivity. They all adapted into a new environment with this collection of four souls bound by several purposes.

These events were possible by the interference of this outsider's trespassing in my presence with her device. Next, they joined in a circle surrounding my family. They were born within the Catholic diocese, these three Christians and one Buddhist/Christian, including an adored queen-to-be using God's powers to control the outcome of the night's events.

They were in my presence not to destroy something, but to expose the truth of her actions, to discover hidden truths that this woman sought after, to formulate a black winged Wiccan king.

Beauty dividing each eyelash melting upon her face, eyeliner collecting in clumps, the spirit of Jacqueline Onassis was in the presence of the fourth wind. Out of the four winds of the universe, her dark brown hair covered her heart of hearts to tell no lies about this shameful nation. Her shame was her secret to be relieved to me later that night.

The second woman was Japanese, as great as the wonders of Mount Fuji. Chi was (Yoko Ono) the power of the eleventh phantasmagoria, who sought after the sights of Lee "the slippery fowl." With her weapon a light that sabers she will bind a friction currently pulls pins to energize magnetic gear plates binding vibrant light with a saber producing a violent beam of energy that discharges barbs that electrocutes with three phase high voltage. Chi halts the Antichrist from awaking the army of the dead that vows to fight against the second coming of the Lord Jesus Christ.

The white stitched curtains blocked the winds and illumination of the sun from crossing that bridge between the living and the dead. Marilyn Monroe did not want demonic spirits to interfere with their search for John F. Kennedy. Her involvement in the prophecies was that her admiration for a person led to her death. Marilyn Monroe knew no such secrets, joining these spirits that night, she cautioned me about the danger around every warning.

The other presence brought together because of Hell, cometh objectives, chronicles Diana's involvement in that night's festivity. It positioned her in front of the harp; her long strife conveyed her emotions with tempest strings. Her absolute adoring affections for the love of God's patrons, the world shivers with blustery winds of radical waves. The vibrations form throughout Diana's vocal cords sorrow out from the entrance in front of her Heavenly home.

I stood back against the wall, listening to the conversations. Like four elderly women playing bridge, it was overpowering to witness, there was a sense of mystery throughout the air—a vortex into other worlds. Like the changing of the barometric pressure that makes a high frequency sound that pierces and pop your ear drums.

They had a distinctive aroma, a scent that penetrated my sinuses. It was intoxicating, bringing me to places I had never seen before. They were graceful, intelligent, and profitable, as they exchanged currency between each other. They were aware that they were together so that I could witness them resurrecting a soul from the hell he was experiencing. Another spirit was lost and was brought to me through the prayers of these four delightful souls.

They all had an objective, a message to deliver that I was to become one of God's most adored Angels. By my oath I deliver the whole truth. The women were in the position to control the wind, and it howled.

The holy cross then had hands laid upon it. They all controlled their winds, their winds meaning the tongues, each word thoughts upon every action. For evil was the force that brought them, love being the bond that forever bound them, mending their hearts eternally as one cluster of colorful sisters.

As they remained silent their lips tightly closed, they were using telepathy to communicate with me. All I knew was they had a purpose that brought them here simultaneously after years of passing.

The four sisters had to keep this woman from achieving her master plan the Presidency, to gather artifacts that Ramon pays dearly for! Bar Jesús needs one book to raise himself and Ramon's mother from the dead. Ramon's mother was another witch who died from a Centurion's blade to the back of her neck after killing his father with a meat cleaver.

His mother's propensity for violence got her head removed late one night by a centurion for worshiping the devil. After the killing of his father, Ramon Cade tress cursed with his mind, madness plagued his thoughts, and uncontrollable words escaped his mouth. Before his mother's death, they placed him within her care, but she knew not how to control his anger. Yet, she was willing to unleash his plague upon the planet. He became a Roman cadet, this Ramon Cade tress.

In this perfect harmony of love, the destination was from inside my mind a battle of telepathy—it is when the Holy Spirit, directed by the Lord Jesus Christ, connects to matter that links us to that great super nova.

A spiritual body holds a living reaction, seen with white noise. The actual thought of movement makes a sound that registers in my mind, body, and soul. When spirits move about, they tend to produce more color and their soul illuminate their features. That becomes a visual illumination within my eyes.

CHAPTER 5

The Sequestered Kennedy

E ach magnificent spiritual body that visited me the night John Kennedy came into my dwelling was very competent. The women had achieved their goal in releasing John's spirit out of the grasp of Satan.

I am proud that my Heavenly Father chose me to guide these four women to resurrect a man, laid to rest long before I was born.

I always remembered his words that rang out over the crowd as his murderers planned in secret to remove that once great speaker. L.B.J. with his private assassin on the roof with nine other shooters, hiding in the sewers and behind the bushes, the old C.I.A agents were ones with Kennedy's blood on their hands.

I begin to think of the day of his assassination as I remember that night. The late Pres. John F. Kennedy Sr. visited me.

As I said, the women had the ability of telepathy. Why should I have uttered a word from my lips? They could hear what I was thinking. They knew that John's presence was not anywhere in the palisade, courtyards, chambers, or planetariums.

John's soul was an asset—a pawn or bishop, perhaps a rook, in this chess match between the forces of light and evil. Satan refused to release him into Heaven and wanted great things in return for his spirit. The women went into battle: they put themselves in harm's way to see this spirit released.

Jackie told me that she had a chance to foresee, and she predicted the horrible things that were about to happen to John on the day of his assassination. After my near drowning, the year before and since, I was made public to a private world. I was then an easier target to monitor because all they had to do was triangulate our position the day I returned from my near drowning.

Everything else made sense when the satellite came online. From my computer, the government spied upon me. At first, it was a test program to keep watch over a runaway child (me). The government was using this program to explain operating protocol, but when the film developed on me, the agency noticed bright lights encompassing my presence. As it was told to me by my grandfather, but I just thought he was having another episode.

I was unable to be a secret for much longer, yet they watched in the interests of injustice—made public as a secret on the democratic secretary's computer. The cabinets were not filled with liquor, but files of black tapes of political families were being whitewashed and closely monitored by satellites.

We were coming into the time of the Armageddon. I was considered a prophetic family of interest, and they watched and observed me, casting lots and placing wages consenting to covenants, pledging false depositions disguising their intentions to cover up the fact that they had violated my civil rights. The cabinets of tape lay dormant, ready for the moment for the files to be deleted, wiping the system clean of any such controversy.

I only say this because when two of our democratic presidents was in office, a woman allowed the satellite to peer into dwellings again and again. She found it comical.

The night Kennedy was in my presence; this woman was on the device because it had sounded an alarm that someone needed to back up the discs and watch what was happening—because I was on a Jacuzzi pointing a gun under my head.

That was the night Jackie, Diana, Marilyn, and Yoko used telepathy in a spiritual gathering to show and tell me the people were spied upon by a very public figure in the private sector.

Now Jackie sat silently in her sackcloth and ashes, only to utter and profess her innocence. Guilt stricken, a result of thoughts placed there by the taunts of wickedness, she felt guilty that her abilities to predict the future could have saved John.

Jackie was afraid of Satan's dark agents coming into the residences. She had a master named Ping with her; she was nervous. The most useful tool of Satan's army is the fear of madness, and I understood that Jackie was plagued with this fear. Angels were not used in this instance, because at that time I was a wild card, an unknown preacher with a checkered past. Angels were not seen because the girls themselves were the only Angels I had needed.

That was a moment in the past when I was receiving secrets that protected our servicemen, officers, schoolteachers, and diplomats. Just remember why Edward Snowden had to leave the country. He told the world that there were most likely more people being spied upon and followed than the government would admit to.

This satellite was put in place to monitor a child of special needs. The government at the time of my birth employed both my grandmother, Clara, and my grandfather.

Meanwhile, Diana was the whisper between two piercing blues, wanting to know the truth about her murderers' involvements, wondering why and how her driver could hold a chauffer's license.

All the spirits there that night played a game of bridge—Diana, Jackie, and Miss Monroe—all knew of each other's involvement. Mr. Lennon, who monitored the night's events from Heaven, triangulated Yoko's spirit to reunite Hell, cometh with her former lover.

Marilyn, the silhouette of my spiritual mother, told me that she relives a nightmare almost every night, where she drives her convertible off the road, traveling down a dark mountainside. She almost loses her head when her throat hits the windshield. Marilyn's brakes failed to stop the convertible from sliding down the mountainside after she packed her belongings, leaving her husband—who happened to be in the Mafia. Of course, this was Marilyn's message to me before she ascended into her Heavenly home, that this was only a nightmare she has sometimes when she sleeps.

Later that night, the light of a dark shadow awakened me. The presence I saw was approximately six feet in height, and he wanted to make Heaven his home. That is why he had come to be with us.

All I could see was the blackness of this man's frame, walking toward the front of the house. I could tell that he was not alive by the sounds from underneath his moans. He grunted with depleted breath, as if he lacked the oxygen to clearly speak to me. Then I also saw that he did not bother to jar a door, and he glided easily into my family's front living room.

Shelly, my youngest daughter was resting on my shoulder and chest. As I un-wrapped her from around my chest, she asked me, deep within her sleep, "Daddy, please don't leave us!" I wanted to stay. Nevertheless, I had to find out why this spirit had bestowed its presence upon us.

After the frightening night of visitation, why was it fascinating, that I could see the spiritual side of life? Either a gift or need of a higher power, the ticket-tape parade that preceded John was running straight through our bedroom gliding out toward the front door on the bottom floor of our house.

I had been living in the house in Jungle Prada, two blocks from the sea. I believed that energy is the spiritual aura that emits from the silhouette of a soul that I saw gliding past the mirrors in our living room. I was accustomed to and aware of the sixth, seventh, eighth, and ninth senses of nature after smell, touch, taste, hearing, and sight, are telepathy, clairvoyance, telekinesis, and high intelligence. I was called again to battle. My duty and my obligation were to grow wiser in the ways of spiritual chanting and the use of prophetic talents. Now that I was alone, I made my way toward John.

The people inside the house were restless, and the air was stale with the smell of dusty old newspapers blowing like leaves down the hall. The breeze coming off the back of this man's head smelled of gunpowder. He requested a driver with authority, as if he was used to people acting on his command. Therefore, I did as ask. "Deliver me to the base and I will tell you, my stories." John said.

I grabbed my keys to my white Chevy Nova off the tail of a pink flamingo lamp while I jammed a pack of cigarettes into my pocket. The ocean's breeze started coming into a trough, causing fog to move in from offshore to the coastline that night. I could see the lights from his presence waiting for me in my car.

Strangely, there were no other spirits or presences with us. I sensed that there was no evil encompassing us either. It was as if Satan had lost the game and was releasing his prisoner from his control. John became too much weight for him to drag around. Satan was not able to avoid an attack from God's Angels, and so he released John. The women had done their work earlier that night, and now God's blessing was this man's presence.

I rolled myself another cigarette, lighting it as I walked out the door. I felt like Heaven was waiting for me in the car. I got into my vehicle. I asked him to buckle up because we were going for a ride. At this point, I was unsure of the reason for John's arrival that night. He requested that I drive him to U.S. Central Command.

I can remember his smile as he interacted with me, he looked like a man just freed from prison. His silhouette was that of a figure in a sharp designer suit. He asked me if he was in America. I thought I had imagined this at first, but many reasons led me to believe this was real because of the stories he told.

I found out more about the spirits that entered through my eyes, affecting my life. This gift was causing massive headaches, a curse of the trait. No medication in the world could stop these stories from happening.

Why should I stop this gift when it was destined to change the course of my life and the eternal outlook on honoring my Heavenly Father? This experience with John Kennedy was a start for me in the use of messaging as a prophet.

However, it was hard to form thoughts into words as these images presented themselves to me. How many more reasons should I have to be in the presence of this great and humble friend? He was as immaculate as his children! He stood eight feet tall. By my standards, I am only 5'5" on tile floor. Yet he walked this world as a giant!

This was the former United States president, John Fitzgerald Kennedy, shot dead on November 22, 1963. John was laid to rest in an unmarked grave, the man in Arlington Cemetery is a Dallas police officer shot dead to switch Kennedy's body for his, to maintain the theory of a single gun assassin.

Besides the conspiracy theory on who was responsible for Kennedy's assassination. Per the BBC the United States government has been infiltrated by the Illuminate. I will never accuse anyone or tell everything I know about Kennedy's assassination, time to move on.

I tried my best to explain a nightmare that John had about his sister as soon as he released John from Satan's grasp. This reflection was not going anywhere until I delivered that package to the base. Why? I guess it was for him to have a chance to tell me his history. He said his son's soul was lost. Somewhere among all Johnnies' literary findings leaves him sublime to this world.

While John asked me to drive to the local air force base in Tampa, he was not able to leave the hallowed ground of my grandmother's former residence or the confines of my car. Releasing John meant that I needed to gain excess to Mac Dill Air Force Base, U.S. Central Command no exceptions.

This country founded on Christianity makes it almost impossible for evil to penetrate God's fortresses. There is no Gestapo waiting for him here. We have many strong spiritual warriors from the world's wars who are awaiting his arrival when God's Angels can collect their packages.

Without a question, I started my way to U.S. Central Command. I thought that it was a usual destination especially after the 9/11 attacks. I was fully aware that this Nova was no Coda, and I most definitely was not Albert Einstein.

I could see the wound, the opening, the blast to the back of this president's head, flashing off the back half of his missing skull, the oil-like darkness dripping down the freshly prim designer suit.

(Caution: Wait for complete interpretation of this nightmare John told me about before passing judgment.)

John Kennedy seemed distraught and exhausted. He told me about a recurring nightmare. He wanted me to interpret this dream and to convey it to others. This dream was about how he felt to be a big brother. The dream started something like this:

Jack and Jill's disheartening sermon

Jack and Jill walked up the hill thirsting for glasses of cold water. Jack sat down, and Jill started to frown. Jack asked, "What's the tall tale, little sis?" Jill shouted out, "Jack, your zipper is down. What an embarrassing moment this is.

What should I do?" All Jack could say was, "If you can plainly see, I have my hands full of drinking water!"

Jill reached over in an instant she zipped Jack right back up. Then unexpectedly, their father came from around the corner and snatched Jack up, hitting him, explaining this sin was of alcohol and the effects of that crazy weed.

He then threw Jack's sister, Jill, in the middle of a cornfield where she started to beg, kneeling at her father's feet. He reached over and struck her across the face. She could not get away, and he grabbed some thread and a couple of bobby pins. As she failed to render a guilty verdict, he called her "a little hornet sleaze." (It breaks my heart even now to I retell this message via dream.)

He placed pins in her body and imprisoned her soul with them inside the pasture on Camp Kennedy for perverting his son's picnic party. Jill was secured by thread and sewed into a canvas, and her body had turned into a Raggedy Ann doll. Jill was crucified because of her act of plain kindness.

Jack was led away, whimpering, "That is not any old Raggedy Ann doll to me! That is my good-luck dragon! Papa, please! Hear me speak when I say this to you. I will be one of your finest presidents someday. Please, that is my sister, she deserves to be reprieved!" (The reality of this event is that John Kennedy's sister, Rosemary Kennedy, was lobotomized by her father (Joe Kennedy) and confined to a wheelchair for most of her life).

Then there was a flashback to the motorcade, as if talking to me was like conversing with an old wartime friend. John was in a state of hysterics as he told the personal story contained in his dreams. Who could blame him? It was an odd and horrible nightmare!

He said, "My own wife Jackie, the mother of my children, knew the night before, yet did nothing. She knew there was more than the ninth gunman on the grassy null.

It was more like a teenager positioned in the sewer like a vermin that shot the final blow."

As John said, "It was like a bad drug deal that went bad. Jackie served her purpose by remaining a grateful pillar of strength as she realized that Bobby was shot dead. Marilyn was the next bountiful beauty that wound up with her medication glued to her fingertips. Jackie could not resist running away."

He said, "That unbelievable woman had a feeling I was going to be shot that morning and ultimately got inside the car! She kissed me as if she was kissing me off or saying good-bye. Like handing me a Dear John letter, within five sensational moments of that half-beaten horror of a church, my son called his mother and stood bravely in battle better than any soldier in Vietnam. God bless her for she knew not what she did. She knew it before it happened because she possessed a gift!"

Was it the scorn of John's repulsive rumored acts and behaviors, or was it some political 'witch hunt' that started back before the signing of the Declaration of Independence? This is what led John to his murderers.

The Kennedy curse was the result of the evil that sailed over from Cuba. With only enough room between the planks of the ship to hide this witch's skull, they could hear her many voices.

One more nail placed in her coffin should have secured the spike through her heart, her skull placed face first in the sack of soiled oats, her torso thrown in with pigs, her hands and feet brought to us by way of stumps.

The first evil sent to us was a witch, rushed to us by the wings of stinging bees and the cackle of fellows chanting her every song, causing the sailors' fatigue to drift them into a deep sleep, throwing their corpses overboard.

Since then, her spirit made it through, causing chaos, screaming while inciting anger inside the walls of the men, making agreements of peace while in a time of war, the wars in Heaven, the battle between rights and wrongs.

More than this, the witch's cackles were to render aggression between the opposing fathers. Sucking the life out of faithful servants all along the frontier until an Angel of Light came along, capturing this burden, casting her into hell for her tithing had not yet been paid and the constitution had not been signed.

The mystery that fell upon that family, and why it was John who had to take a shot like that, who knows the truth since they seldom speak of it? Jackie stood near a window as John became a martyr. She knew the danger that awaited John Jr. around each corner. What could she do?

When she replaced him, it was the time she was to be creative with another parcel. Christina Onassis was a gifted Angel who was admired by many for her courage and her braveries. God had blessed this world with such an audacious woman. What an intelligent pick. I find my visions of these young women surreal. She had the righteousness that can bring most men to their knees.

Before these fears become our worst reality, a life about horrors, people being tortured by wicked people silenced from the fear of their opposition. Yet much of people wise enough to speak have gags placed upon their hearts. We need a voice stern enough to shake men to their feet. I will serve my purpose for her, or any other person, to take what was rightfully given to me, and give back to the world.

Be wise, for in the days to come it may be impossible to distinguish the government's true intentions from its dark ulterior motives. The Antichrist will be present in the world when the world is not working in unison, and on that day, he will relieve my sister's descendants of her loot to control the planet by winning a world election. This powerful dictator will be an influential speaker who will capture millions of people's attention, while disguising his true intentions to control the universe.

The wound visible, the sight of this president's spiritual presence was like looking at a soul magnified by ten times the father's weight. To see John's face, light up like 50,000 candle watts of power ascending throughout his soul. That made him appear with such clarity to me. He was brilliant and regretful for not always maintaining righteousness, because the chaos after his assassination gave Satan's angels a chance to capture him.

My eyes filtered out the pixels made out by the light, looking within a beam of colors fading into black and white. I guess the moon, or the tide must have played an effect on the ghostly arrival. This conversation seemed to have no timeline, as I was visioning the events from his perspective. We had not made it yet to U.S. Central Command.

I have always been true to business. I am always ready to take a journey for God, even if it lands me in jail, and I am forever ready to call upon God's Angels. I was to be a protector of the peace, a treasurer of memories, and a voracious refuge of the last siege.

The wound lay open on the back of this president's head, oil-like blood slicking down the back of his shirt, covering the rear of his trousers with more blood and confetti. John lived a noble life, but why did he have to die?

I appreciate the Kennedy family's service to their country and the true blood spilt defending freedom and the republic. How much more nobility do you need? Are there actions before death that make a man noble or is it what he says before he cries out? Heaven is calling for a witness.

John Jr. will be that prince someday, as Tupac shall raise his cane and salute his king. A vice president to be, if the purpose is to elect a golden God, then those two will be twins, for our colors are waves upon our flags, colors that stand for more than black, white, red, yellow, or brown.

Everyone represented and laid to rest side by side beneath our father's breast is where our eagles keep their young. You shall not find racism within the hearts of my young ones, for we were born of lionesses, made to live like zebras, while our monarch protects us from the jackals of this world.

After I had heard all, I needed to hear, I turned off the road named in his honor and started our way to Mac Dill Air Force Base, known as U.S. Central Command. We arrived at the base and denied access twice. If on the third time we did not make it to the grounds of the military base, I don't know what would have happened to put his spirit into position. It was God's will for me to pull up to the property of the base long enough for me to release my cargo.

John needed a military airlift command flight to Washington DC or Navarro, Texas. The adventure with John was something that occurs rarely. My years of spiritual chanting brought many spirits to my presence seeking salvation and deliverance. I was becoming a resource to the spirits that did not know all the rules granting them entrance into Heaven's gate or a place in purgatory to avoid a sentence in hell. I followed Kennedy's request to deliver him to the base and we did succeed.

CHAPTER 6

Vision of the Darkest Day

The third time I pulled up to the gate at Mac Dill Air Force Base, I got lucky. A female guard asked me what was in the trunk of my Nova. I answered her question with,

"A shark, one dead body, a skim board, and a couple of men's fashion magazines." I guess I piqued her curiosity. She asked me to pull up into the inspection lane.

We had to be invited in. I was not afraid of being arrested. The fact of the matter is that I have seen far too many miracles happen, as I have witnessed many things because of having been detained. Because of the importance of this mission, I did not ask any questions. I needed no explanation. At this point, I did need some sleep and wanted to go to bed.

I guess my words were enough to warrant a full body search. I exited the vehicle. She opened the trunk while my cargo, my friend for the last hour, vanished from the premises. She then informed me that if I were to return to the base, she would call the local police.

Now that the Nova was clear of my delivery, I sat in that inspection lane having visions and forewarning solutions to prolong the rise of the Antichrist. I saw that love, compassion, sympathy, understanding of great wealth would prove to the Heavenly Father that this manuscript could make people see the light through the eyes of a gifted man.

Interpretations of biblical scrolls instruct apostles to delegate the Archangels to deliver and relay God's commands. The legion of Angels sacrifices their sinful predecessors, cleansing themselves with holy water and the eternal fire of the Holy Spirit. This means that by now, the position assigned, the battle raged, and it is over. So, talk to Jesus about a spiritual rebirth as an angel in His army.

If that armed guard at Mac Dill Air Force Base only knew what kind of vision, I was having the moment that package been delivered. Christ's apostles have told me that the evolution of humankind prolongs the timeline of the rise of the Antichrist. We have some control over that destiny. My feeling is that within two to fifty decades, the coins at the gambling table will fall, and Ramon will change the odds on every wager ever placed by him.

Remember when I stated in "Angel's Message" that Lucifer split into two? That is what he does here with Bar Jesús and Elías they are the same person that splits into two people, controlled by Lucifer, that becomes Ramon Cade tress. In the end he may again falsify his name to condemn any preconceived notion of what his whereabouts are.

Satan has said on more than one occasion that he will walk this earth in the spirit, in the spiritual body, and in the flesh at one given time. Our Heavenly Father's son, Jesus Christ, is the monumental Trinity in Heaven and on Earth.

When the Father in Heaven made His son and then created the Holy Spirit, He in return gave man back three crucial aspects of humanity. Made in His image, the Heavenly Father gave us mind, body, and soul. Satan wished to obtain greatness, and he likes that everybody knows him. People never forget his names. To the wicked ones in question, I ask, what service have you performed for the Lord Jesus Christ today? Just to test the spirit.

Satan will have many more opportunities to attempt his triumph victory against the Heavenly Father, yet however shrivels in shame at His feet; Satan will be too small for Him to battle, too afraid to face Jesus Christ whose spiritual body is Hector of Troy.

Satan waits until the day that Lucifer has no more bodies left to disguise himself into his final human form.

Then he will face Jesus Christ's magnificent benevolent powers. Satan presents himself to Christ, submissive and remorseful like he was at the beginning. Because the result of his punishment is chained within a cage in a parallel dominion trapped and incarcerated in the depths of the Earth, his dying hell.

My vision was of a newspaper headline: *What We Lost to the World Today!* In the news were the beginnings of forewarnings and speeches of a communist crowd, saying that God's descendants could save the world by bringing serenity and peace to change the planet. That terrible birth depends upon our ignorance.

We should not ignore the Savior because it may be too late for us to repent. The world expects chaos! Let us be bearers of peace; we can change this world. We are led by corporations instead of by the people electing representatives who defend high morals standards in the middle of our Republic.

This Antichrist will not breed. He will be sterile like a donkey and brood having offspring. He knows the "word" yet will push people from it. Hatred for this world is what this monster wishes to bring to his pulpit, always walking with a limp, present with cane—you know the drug.

One way to diminish his strength is to develop a usable and sustainable source of energy. He wants our precious pearls, and the pearls of wisdom contain the knowledge of how to do this with atomic energy and cold fusion. If this does not stop the beast from rising, find a solution to some of the world's problems.

The antichrist wants the throne of England. It strikes fear in the land and control by total domination of the entire planet. He was close to being born when Hitler rolled his tanks above the ground. Knowing now what we must conquer, his skin lay dry as silt. His suit had been placed out, dusty with much debris. His cabin is somewhere behind Europe, bordering Russia, as a vinyl music box plays tunes of another language with enticing sounds.

Noticing it is not his time by the tune that is playing on that record station; communistic sounding speeches, while wailings of anti-Semitism will be the signs that will make this curator start to sing. Waiting for the time, the suit will make rhyme with reasons, nothing to do other than murdering sounds with his false preaching.

Let us recreate and produce what we have the most of; that is, water. Food and drinking water will become a scarce commodity. If we don't work on a solution to our global energy problem, we will see real terror sooner rather than later. The Lord Jesus Christ will destroy all evil in the universe, while the filth that the beast needs will breathe.

We can stop this beast from forming, creating a longer timeline, by loving each other, bringing ourselves forward, preaching the words each day. Live within your Holy Temple, allowing your heart to be your guided way.

Satan's spawn will be born as Bar Jesús Elías Caduceus aka Ramon Cade tress, yet his will and his manner of thinking begot by his intentions, full of gambles saturated with many risks. He is a servant only to himself. He will try to persuade the masses to surrender to him as a superior Christ.

Bar Jesús will serve and sacrifice from underneath the hands of God before serving himself. He will attempt to defy God's laws claiming the Lord Jesus Christ has no power. Only a select group will become God's Heavenly Angels. Both Bar Jesús and Lucifer have been removed from that honor.

In the gospel of Luke, the apostle gave the story behind the name of Bar Jesús Elías Caduceus. The story is that the devil presented himself to a man at the crucifixion of the Lord Jesus Christ's. The man promised enormous powers in exchange for his soul and committed sorcery on behalf of the Jewish people a close friend of Caiaphas. After that, the Roman cadet stabbed Jesus Christ's lung with his spear. They witnessed Judas's suicide and, again, Satan entered Judas' body to mock the apostle.

And Satan entered Judas Iscariot, one of Jesus' twelve apostles. (Luke 22:3 NCV)

Bar Jesús was promised greatness below the tree of betrayal, as Judas's body swayed. Bar Jesús viewed the spear of destiny as majestic since, Longinus a centurion that stabbed Jesus and Jesus' blood spray back into his one blind eye and was healed. Bar Jesús wanted to wheel that kind of power, fled with Satan to higher grounds, as the Lord Jesus Christ's resurrected His body walked among His followers.

There will be far more at stake than what is here on Earth. This planet is the most critical property in our galaxy. The war in the Heaven above rages on, and I am here to witness it firsthand. The Antichrist will be an immoral being, the son of the devil in a three-piece suit. Bar Jesús was given the name Ramon Cade tress from then on to his last breath, he knew he would rebuke anyone else praising Jesus' name.

When Ramon least expects it, it will be his lack of faith that will turn God's fury into masses of people seeking Ramon's removal of political office. While in the time of great suffering, the reckoning will happen when the presence of the Antichrist has his foothold throughout the world. Then, people will begin to prepare for the events that will cause the world to shake.

If the people that are survivors, they are chosen to be witnesses or left to nurture back to health this once shaken planet. If the rest of the world survives or dies by the fires of hell, as this planet will then be consumed by fire, then the light shall dawn on you in your day, and the Almighty Son shall reign for a thousand God-years.

We need to keep cleansing the earth. I hope you enjoy your life, return yourself to worship, praise God you're free. When our time in Heaven is finished, legions of Angels will come to comfort the sick and reclaim what is rightfully God's the earth and our souls.

We as Angels shall be in the final stages of discharging the chosen out of hell while releasing them into the universe. The kingdom of God will have all the glory in the universe, and the Lord Jesus Christ shall have control over every chamber in your heart.

In moments of time, numbers will reveal the increments of this planet's involvement in wars of worship, our first proper line of defense. I had vowed to say that our importance in Satan's advancement is for us to hold our litigations until after the boundaries breach.

Be silent, hear me, and listen. When the Antichrist reigns, he will pour wickedness onto us. We had better be full of grace at the time of his arrival.

The crowds will war one last time. The concept of how all things created, and all known intelligence, exist in him. He shall not serve a lighter sentence in hell for the terrible things this son of darkness has spat upon the people of this planet.

Then, shall he say also unto them on the left hand, depart from me, ye cursed, into everlasting fire, prepared for the devil and his angels. (Mt 25:41 KJV)

I have been there. I have seen the Antichrist's plan to leave this world after its destruction into space with his ship. He will be descending on a path surviving when resurrected.

In other words, his body will be shot out to the outer space on a rocket. The hope is that someone or something will breathe life back into his soul. Trust in this Antichrist and all you shall perish from God's presence forever. Choose to be a servant of God. Watch your fortunes multiply quite heavily.

Let your trust in God strengthen your footing. As Ramon holds dusty horns that shall never play an even tune, he shall live in the land of the mountains while burning his feet in quicksand.

Ramon will quote scripture until his rules are all undone, and his spoken words are all, but broken. God's will be to sacrifice him for the evil deeds he has been causing throughout the course of his creation.

It was Bar Jesús, with the help of Satan, who took the gift of foresight to use for his dark purposes. His supremacy will soon be at hand. Ramon will release unmerciful spirits placed upon his mantle in hell, souls Satan and His Angels of darkness collected throughout the creation of man.

When that new day comes, we will not be caught off guard. We will graciously wait in eternity for the day that war may rage once more in Heaven. We shall know and be prepared for it.

Ramon could place a rock to fall before a price, and then grab the wager before the pebble stopped rolling. Half his fortunes were made through a large and well-known corporation owned and run by the Illuminate.

Having the gift of foresight, trust me, he is gambling with far more by the end of all time. It will be property, gold, and artifacts that Jesus Christ is willing to give to him in the place of something as precious as a human soul.

The Lord Jesus Christ's entire spiritual splendors connect us with His all-powerful beam of light (The Holy Spirit). Your will must be as close to the Lord Jesus Christ's as humanly possible to bind together to create one large weapon that the beast will not be able to resist or to walk away from. He has lost his battle before it even began.

The outcome of this war will rage on, and if he gains his footing, he could control the outcome of this planet. Bar Jesús desires everything perishable to perish until the earth is made whole again. Then there could be a chance that life could start back at square one—another Adam and Eve.

The key is Confucius. All I can do is to sit across from him in the time that Satan and his demonic angels break-through their chains, scaling the gates of hell. Satan will attempt to overthrow our government, again and again. This chance is as good as our last, so it is imperative that we must succeed.

What I have seen after the return of Jesus Christ is rogue angels crucified, many crosses lining a lake of fire, (the Gulf) as many were Archangels defeating by the Trinity the army of Lucifer's lost and forgotten angels of darkness. Many angels captured in this last siege for the ultimate control over Heaven.

After exclaiming my quietus, then mounting my cross, I will suspend myself in the absolute vacuum of space, until time becomes a continuum. I wanted to symbolize my savior ecclesiastically speaking, by mounting my cross, with holes for the nails that penetrate my limbs, levitating my angelic body upon my crucifix.

This struggle will continue even after the world incinerates, and there are few, if any, souls left on earth. Humanity has one chance to save humanity—that is, we cannot allow Hell, cometh into the White House again. That is a big mistake!

No one knows our fate because humans can evolve, gaining wisdom from the wise, while learning from past mistakes. We can anticipate the battle before it happens. We should know before he rises what he can do. We should look clearly at his maniacal plan.

The grass, sour and rotten on his patch of the pasture, the fields are flat, littered with bunkers, many boulders and decaying vegetation due to nuclear rain. The only good things that will grow are potatoes.

Ramon's life will perish because of his taunts consumed by his lies, built upon the illusion of what the universe will be like under his father's command (Satan). We should be grateful because of the Lord Jesus Christ's sacrifice, His power, and His wisdom. We all might have had to die upon the cross.

After all this, that superior being will exist. This Antichrist is another dark angel in human form. He will live life as a warlock. If we are lucky to avoid nuclear war, then we should not have to worry about where this being has planned for his reign on the parade.

The antichrist's last actions will be spitting vile while his skin burns in the presence of the Almighty Son, the Lord Jesus Christ. His flesh will crust like bread, yet will not flake, not one particle of his matter, will remain in our universe.

Within that moment, his heart stops beating, each chamber exploding as the souls most precious to him dissolved from our presence. Levitating chained crucifix, collared, and pending his quietus, Ramon will be scared half to death with the thought of crucifixion.

Placed shortly to appear in a galactic stadium in front of Our Heavenly Father with the multitudes of Angels present with their lights and sabers, with bibles in hand, as the Lord Jesus Christ prepares the Antichrist and Satan, etc., for hell.

The panel of judges will chain him in irons made of all his dastardly deeds, he then transforms into the beast known to believe only in himself. A once lost now captured angel will await sentencing, ready to journey into the center of the earth for the last time to smell what he has created.

"Then the devil, that had deceived them, was thrown into the fiery lake of burning sulfur, joining the beast and the false prophet. There they will be tormented day and night forever and ever." (Rev 20:10 KJV)

Back at the base, the soldier woman was waiting for me to come out of my catatonic state, so she could return my keys to me as I sat inside my Nova. I started to drive myself away. With the charges placed on my wife, this story will continue through the separation of our marriage. As I watched my marriage brew in turmoil, it was the adventure after the marriage that led the FBI and CIA hot on my tail.

Due to the origin of my birth, the fact of my conception placed me on a government hot list. Watching me far before the nation disregarded my civil liberties, before the offices had a proper warrant to scan me over thoroughly. Why, I don't know.

These trials saved my life, giving me purpose after Josephine left. By this time, Jesus Christ contested my sins and breathed a new relevance within my repentance. He then set my soul free, as I honored my atonement and conquered sin through my salvation. He charged me with being a bringer of peace, understanding, and an abundance of sustenance.

I said in prayer, "Subtle by He is I!" The Lord Jesus Christ simply replied, "Whereby thy side?" The sun in me shone. "You are the reign that binds me." I asked, "Revel in Psalms at this I am to be?" He then replied, "The sums of many sums." I asked him, "Prove this right." He said "fine". So, I paid my fee.

This is Jesus Christ's spoken words to me, and he said, "Cast grains of seeds before my mother's eyes, see if she would shed a star and begin to stow!" or "Cast a pebble upon my Father's fleece, see if light begins to glow!" "Cast a stone at my brother's fleet; see if a well begins to flow." He then placed a hammer in my hands and falling upon two long planks were three long nails given to me from the Lord Jesus Christ's hands. He said this was to create a massive sail for a seaworthy vessel, one large cross strong enough to navigate through the strength of the swirling winds, all in different directions.

We were searching and clearing our mass free of the churning sea, while scattering our planks out into the ocean. Jesus navigates our vessel as we swing from the masses. Without our ship this lesson, without his presence, there is no guide for thee, deprived of our compass, we spin east to west and west to east, counting on the stars to guide us.

Whether you are north of the equator or south of the Yucatan Peninsula, open your mouths to savor the freshness of the water misting off a gentle breeze. His direction keeps you rowing steadily on course from out of the sea, and you have landed yourself upon solid flocks of Angels. In the ocean, you have conquered all sorts of fears. The fact is you are a mariner overcoming your terrors.

CHAPTER 7

Another Parallel

I t was long ago when I fell into the depths of a spiritual depression. I was experiencing visions with deep meditation that took me to places inside my mind—places that I had never seen before, where all people were represented by decks of cards.

Each card played out in the fifth dominion. Each player had a multitude of geometric shapes to their physical appearance, disguises that conceal their soul from their opponent. Each card was a judge, a magistrate, or a counselor in a courtyard of Heaven deep in orbit, in outer or inner space.

Two large granite thrones stood on either side of this courtyard, as each figure performed an action or event, from singing, to dancing, to quoting manuscripts. These courtyards were full of activity with both Angels and travelers from different dominions coming to receive counseling or to obtain direction or even perhaps to play in a game.

Those singing and dancing five-dimensional characters acted out the card games, and with every new level, it was the antes that brought about gaming whales (souls that place large wagers are called whales), from far across the galaxy.

There was no other hand higher than a royal flush, yet it was the hearts that won the battles, the spades that finished wars, and the clubs that carried our prayers. There was a suit especially for the royal families, called spreads. Spreads were the suit of all suits. They won over all suits. They held more weight, carried the burden alone. They were the equivalent of God's wild cards, His secret assassins.

These card games were played by the royals of the elites in these courtyards of Heaven, or within the judges' chambers. They wore black togas, except for their faces, covered with masks made from all types of yard stones, gems and, of course, plastic and metals. The level of play depended on the severity of service, and competence determined the outcome of fame.

I visualized this courtyard while traveling through a vortex of thought. I had the Lord Jesus Christ guiding my vessel. I was planning and trailing through the stars on this quest of knowledge. He was taking me for a ride that took me into the realm of the bird people, past the judicial thrones, into a world all on its own, separated and divided.

To travel from dominion to dominion is a completely different ball of matter. If you could think of this as several different channels, each channel a different form like your own being, performing the same actions as you, yet in a different dominion.

While having the same characteristics of that person, we are made of the same fiber. Each channel is another lifeline in which the person can travel, speaking different languages while living in different locations all throughout the galaxies. We live lives that have already been lived here on earth.

Now I am talking about after the physical death of your mortal body here on earth. After death, you will live each life like a dream. We are like a beam of light that is never broken, just a splendor of your reflection, of your existence throughout eternity, living in a state of perpetual bliss.

It is like having one hundred steps from the bottom of a staircase to Heaven's gate. Each step holds a different form of you, another spiritual body slow to speak. As you take each step, you live each lifetime, as you reach the top of those one hundred forms, you become one entity. You are then compounded together through the power of Christ's ultimate all-powerful being, into your supreme self. I hope I have adequately explained this concept for you.

You will not be held in a three-dimensional form, but you will sit with sixteen different sides in your ninth dimensional spiritual inhabitation. This will enable you to walk by, traveling through vortexes by choosing a corridor.

Millions of paintings cover the walls of these galleries, each picture or portrait holding and having a lifetime of experiences within it. You choose your portrait to live a life and then experience you're greatest.

Remember, eternity is a lifetime of forever compiled with each desire within your imagination, until that sentence is broken, your life in eternity will remain the same livable, breathable existence you have always been accustomed to. Think outside the box!

Living outside tomorrow with a new body, a far superior mind, traveling with the lights that emit from your aura—the heat radiating from your soul—this is the presence of Heaven, and it is how space-travel will exist. It became possible for me to witness the legion of Angels that had been present in bodily form.

I was not much out of place; they were more like interstellar benevolent beings to me. Visited by some of these loved ones from this other planet shortly after Josephine's departure, I was amid their shadows. Seeking justice deep within the chambers of gardens beyond the traveling reach of the spiritual agents known as Nomads.

Nomads were evil's equivalent of prophets. If you ever come across a Nomad, you will know it because they don't have a face: absolutely no eyes, ears, or mouth.

Nomads position themselves at ninety-degree angles, viewing into the corners of your eyes to predict what will happen in your future. So, they can jump out and snatch your blessings while pulling your card right out of the hands of God. Always protect your eyes, for they are like windows that these agents use to predict your future, within your line of sight.

If your eyes are the windows to your soul, then your corneas are the timelines of your life, a mirror image of your destiny. If you are not aware, be aware now. Many bad things happen to good people because they are not aware, and the elders determine how well you handle yourself while they monitor your life experiences. Angels serve either your punishment or blessing. When the time comes that your card is pulled, your number has been called.

Maybe you will get a job, or perhaps you will spill coffee on your suit. As you know, far worse things happen to good people all the time because these events have been predestined.

Wagers of such events played out in those courtyards. In those thrones, the only time there is an upset is when a miracle of God occurs, preventing that tragedy from happening. Kind of like the beautification of the spiritual rebirthing process, perpetuating prior lives. The guardian Angel, Karma has the pleasure of supreme sovereignty over most souls wanting or willing to return to earth. She is virtually flawless.

That is why it is so important to continue a constant dialogue with the Lord Jesus Christ. Profitability is determined by your constant communication with Jesus so that your free will turns into an act of obedience. Wagers are placed by spirits whether you succeed or fail.

After being visited by the goddess the night before, crying my eyes dry in the master's domicile, I prayed for a miracle to step forth in my life, proving that I was worthy of my salt.

I started out on a religious quest that began with a seven-day fast and ended with forty-one days of celibacy. I performed this act to satisfy my curiosities about the commandments that I must obey, that I might obtain grace, making my atonement with God. I found the inner workings of Heaven amusing. I tested my abilities and determined my strengths.

I kept traveling in my dreams to this world parallel to ours, as if God had created this world in case; we fail him by destroying this planet. I found that inside of this world, it is like earth, and although Heavenly it was plagued with many crimes.

A magistrate who was practicing sorcery ruled a corruptible society. He frequented the courtyard in Heaven, causing fights and riots. Yet, on this spiritual planet, primarily covered with forests and trees, there is not the ocean we see.

It had shadows of darkness, doubt plaguing the land, unearthing good soil, replacing the distinct aroma of honey with pure sulfur. There was a distinctive smell for every person. A life of fantasy-like living in self-portraits bases of oils and stains—memorials of memoirs placed within a frame of time.

Traveling in this universe is accomplished with wings. The population of this universal world filled with the presence of families, young children that were once living breathing human beings. They have small-framed bodies, very strong, and petite kind of like a cherub yet, made of white light and in the form of a bird.

These spiritual bird individuals are constantly covering their faces with masks. Many spirits live in this world because of its natural similarities to earth. Rings of radiant light make us believe we are solar collectors, and the illumination belongs eternally with the electricity within our souls. Their land halts time seldom revolves around a star. Their planet must be the force of gravity. Yet, there is an evil presence and his son.

The spiritual name of Bar Jesús is the title given to an Anunnaki angel that will inhabit this portrait as the false prophet of the superior Antichrist, he is very wicked. His adopted father is a high-ranking official for Satan himself and a sorcerer his false prophet.

Bar Jesús or the name I knew him as Ramon Cade tress traveled to my presence on more than one occasion to cast lots and place wagers. He had with him many evil spirits that caused violent things to happen to the other spirits that were visiting me from that distant planet. That resulted in me cutting my wrist to make the chaos stop and for Ramon to leave my visitors alone.

Nevertheless, Ramon has been defeated many times. They both kind of stay out of my providence ever since Gabriel's encounter Satan splitting into two, while her legion covered all bases. They made the sky so bright that sundown was an hour late.

As I traveled to this world, the first thing I was to do was to use the Word of God to speak the truth to their masses. The people from this distant planet understood that I had a supreme quality to add to this distinct native language.

Each one of us has many rubber suits and many job titles in this spiritual world. Our duties determined by the acts finished and performed by us for God in our current lifetime here on earth.

There are dangers in this world that threaten the thoughts or perceptions on the way life should be. I redeem and validate their existence. They said I was one of the few who communicated with their species through mental mediation.

The fall of one person was the cause of chaos—a murderer in this spiritual world. The spirit I speak of is Bar Jesús's adopted father, a sorcerer from a different dominion the Antichrist's prophet Elías both them unrighteous and unholy with one body with split personalities. If you look up the meaning of his name, you will find that it is a time after the Heaven's creation.

KJV (Acts 13:8-12) "[8] But Elías the sorcerer (for so is his name by interpretation) withstood them, seeking to turn away the deputy from the faith. [9] Then Saul, (who also is called Paul,) filled with the Holy Ghost, set his eyes on him. [10] And said, O full of all subtilty and all mischief, thou child of the devil, thou enemy of all righteousness, wilt thou not cease to pervert the right ways of the Lord? [11] And now, behold, the hand of the Lord is upon thee, and thou shalt be blind, not seeing the sun for a season. And immediately there fell on him a mist and a darkness; and he went about seeking some to lead him by the hand. [12] Then the deputy, when he saw what was done, believed, being astonished at the doctrine of the Lord."

Many of our leaders, without knowing, change the outcome of events in this spiritual world. They cause our timeline to shift the balance of this planet. In this parallel Universe, Ramon, was hung out to dry, has been defeated.

I held proof to this event after the Archangel Gabriel visited me. When she confronted me, she was in the form of a woman again. Gabrielle is a far greater warrior as male or female, and she was glowing, stunning, and radiant. The Archangel Gabrielle battled Satan as Bar Jesús, Elías, known as Ramon all three names the same person with multiple minds, spoke to Gabrielle about the completion of this book.

Gabriel came back to my location after the battle was finished and told me that, through my prayers; the army of bird people defeated Bar Jesús and arrested his adopted father Elías. The bird-people established a new government and placed Elías in prison for practicing sorcery. One of the three spirits Ramon portrayed left his suit and disappeared from that planet. In other words, his body had descended into the universe to avoid capture.

I spent much time in meditation with these bird-like people. When they removed their masks in my presence, eyes wide open, they were pure white light. The suits they had on were made of a rubber-like material, allowing them flight throughout the universe. I came upon a wheel in this parallel universe that has several different characters placed like granite statues upon it.

There was something I was searching for since Josephine left. I was on a voyage to find my spiritual mate. I found a lot of empty pages, yet non full of surprises. I might share my heart, having salvation, and among my play, the burden of serenity, to ploy this supremely chosen one out from her shadows.

Within rare moments of my life, some brides have entered, but only she has won my heart's deepest affections. Standing there on that round granite platform stood their statues, surrounded by the men I always wanted to be growing up. Statues of the following people presently carved memorializing their existences:

The queen of all queens, my forever-lovely queen of hearts, had the features of a goddess grandchild of Abraham and Queen of her own Galaxy, Carrie Underwood; the promises of eternal life featuring Whitney Houston placed on this round tablet closely resembling a large sundial, placed in a green pasture on the outside the city light overlooking this burg like town.

Instantaneously they began to sing, for the crowds congregated in my presence, with their magical man with his love for God and Country, Tim McGraw.

Standing beside the United States Constitution the pillars between each cornerstone, the marquees above his head, a demigod, half man, half godly individual in justice for-ever we crawl to the feet of President Donald J. Trump. His entire families are truthsayers, magnanimous, Angelic, Demigod's.

The twin towers—those curls with their beauty at first glance, never a second look—were the Olsen twins. They are to be the daughters of a titan, and empresses they shall be.

The hermit manmade invisible with his mystical capes and his adopted granddaughter, Jessie, looked like Sean Connery and Athena Onassis.

The monkey man mimicking an ape swinging from a tree was my adopted father, Papa Callicoat. The centurion father was Arnold Schwarzenegger.

There was the father of many and emperor of his own universe, Mel Gibson and, of course, there I was—a childlike demigod protégé— sitting amongst tombstones, with flowers growing past my knees. Surrounded by these features carved out of granite statues, the sunsets were awesome, always different colors of pastel sunbursts setting my hair ablaze.

There is the mother to all that spares the switch when it comes to delegating our chores. Oprah Winfrey is a monumental image of our eternal mother. She has vested stock in every young one born within her borders.

Of course, there is Paris Hilton, my unicorn, and Kourtney Kardashian—what a wonderful person and hottest of the sisters—and of course, one of the greatest mothers on earth, Kris Jenner.

Bruce Jenner aka Caitlyn Jenner, I just want you to know that in Heaven we can be both male and female at any given moment. It is a lifetime of forever living throughout eternity living lives past and future tales as mom, dad, brother, sister, grandma, and granddad, connected by one beam of light traveling all throughout the Universe displayed.

Now this next woman's voice captured my presence—upon this monument, her image carved into the stone. I guess they were there pairing you with your eternal spiritual mate. In this vision, I could see the reflections of sunsets, shadows of those eyes. Falling in love with her was like melding two souls, harmoniously bound throughout the depths of eternity.

The fact is this gifted woman, brings smiles to the innocents of faithful children with that magnificent face just by singing hello. I have immortalized her presence because she bared her soul to me through her lyrics to these parallel worlds.

She is an angel that gave me a glimpse of her heart within her music: Amy Lee from Evanescence! That is why we should surrender to the soul of our spirit to obtain the will of God and promises of eternal life in

Heaven. These people have touched my soul, and my life is affected by their presence here on earth.

Visited by spirits of a different time, many more famous people come to me as Angels, they have spent time with me after their deaths: Dr. Martin Luther King Jr.; Howard Hughes, Patrick Swayze; Michael Jackson; Elon Musk's Knighthood, Elvis Presley; Heath Ledger; Bernie Mac; Sterling Holloway was Winnie the Pooh; Walt Disney; Robin Williams, John F. Kennedy Sr.; John Kennedy Jr.; Tupac Shakur; Jon Banét Ramsey; Anna Nicole Smith; John Lennon; Silvia Brown; Kurt Cobain; Bruce Lee; DJTJr. Michael Clarke Duncan, Whitney Houston, David Carradine; Diana, Princess of Wales; Brittany Murphy, Albert Einstein; Thomas Edison; L. Ron Hubbard; Nicola Tesla, Marlon Brando; Jacqueline Onassis; James Gandolfini; Paul Walker; John Ritter, Chris Cornell and Seth Rich.

CHAPTER 8

The Decoding of God's Messages

I was not sure of the path that my thoughts should have taken, my mind tracing the courses of different galaxies and other watery solar systems. I was having constant dreams that these worlds will be annihilated by warfare.

I was hoping and praying that my writing will lead me to a different outcome. I wanted to convince you that humankind could make a difference in determining an alternate result. I did not want to think about the grim reminder that earth will be consumed by fire.

No question that the oceans will freeze when the earth's ozone depletes, but first the sun releases its magnetic field, and the planets will rotate into outer space.

That is when all the water in the world evaporates as the earth falls from orbit. The final location of what use to be earth is designed to be re-inhabited in a vacuum from outer space.

By then we will have the technology to travel with the earth's trajectory. There will be another ice age, and the oceans will freeze, when there is no more oxygen and the earth become dry and barren there will be small pods of people on planet earth. Finding another watery planet that supports life will be a number one priority. When and how is the big question?

This led me to three theories: an imploding star emits a gamma ray burst that sends radiation throughout the galaxy; a large meteor from a location in the universe called wormwood strikes the earth; and lastly. The devil takes on multiple human forms and finishes the destruction he started many millennia ago by launching and detonating several nuclear warheads on the outskirts of a nuclear holocaust. My perspective is that man is primarily good; an act of God's will be to accomplish our tasks here on earth.

The good thing about a gamma ray burst is you will never know when it happens. Occurring at a supersonic rate of speed, the earth's surface will vaporize before you have a chance to cry out for help!

Another conspiracy that I have recently been made aware of is the book of Enoch. The fact that he was the grandfather of Moses he was a colored man with white hair. He wrote this manuscript before Genesis. In Genesis it states that the scripture in the book of Enoch is prophetic, but I digress. It states that the earth is a flat surface as the sun and moon revolve around the North Pole as the center of the surface. Like an alternate Universe the plains that God conceives as fact that He looks at our world as a flat plain rather than a circular surface.

Called the firmament the distance from the surface of the earth to the Heavens is twelve hundred kilometers, the distance between the surface of the earth and the ability to drill is twelve hundred kilometers. Why can't we drill deeper than twelve hundred kilometers?

Why can't some commercial fights fly direct routes to certain Continents? Because of the mountains and oceans, the flight must have layovers and alternate passages. Is the distance to great or is it because we are flying a radius instead of a straight line? I think the Book of Enoch is prophetic yet is inaccurate. I think if the earth is flat, it is still in a shape of a circle that makes us believe it is round.

The government has hidden the fact that space travel may not be possible, that we only occupy space in the outer atmosphere. This could not be truer then, space exploration, could not be as that the earth appears around because the sun only shone around image into one dimensional camera, everything else is digitally enhanced to mislead us. Just the way Satan wants it the world believing in falsehoods just like this one. We are not worshipping God the creator and his Son Jesus Christ, are we?

I don't worry about acts of God. The worst global destruction that we should be concerned about is nuclear war—when there are survivors to this horrible event. Left to live like slaves as this country falls under the control of foreign lords.

Unless I can somehow inspire you to evolve and let me help, you save our planet! First, Hell, cometh cannot become president. She would start the one-hundred-year foot war, where our soldiers walk street to street, policing cities of Ukraine and the Middle East. She will destroy all our allies, which will leave us in isolation. The constitution must change to a one-union country under God's (command).

There will be only one party, an independent nation of God's (people). Patriots

Many things must occur before these apocalyptic events will take place, like a world leader making peace with Israel, and Jerusalem beginning to rebuild its temple.

All this happens as the Lord Jesus Christ's anointment in Heaven causes the Holy Spirit to deliver to the faithful widespread miracles of healing. Angel Raphael.

The world's leaders end up with all that oil and no one to sell it to. Cost of gas and refinery rises. As we switch to electric cars.

We must avoid the civil wars and riots, famine and plagues, the pestilence that runs rapidly throughout the lands.

I was told these things could be avoided. First, the United States must come up with a new energy conservation method.

Subatomic nuclear fusion is a device delivered to me by benevolent sources; it is a viable solution to our energy crisis.

When our energy costs range close to $300 billion annually, the solution to this expense is subatomic nuclear fusion. We should open our minds to the possibility that an ordinary person might hold the patent and have the answers to our strife. We must comprehend the solution that I have written in this autobiography—that an absorption device on a monumental scale could produce a new branch in energy savings, and we should not depend on fossil fuels. Instead burn greenhouse gases as an alternative fuel keeps us warm, even on the dark and dreary nights.

Why not try it? There is nothing to lose. Visions I have received here lately is an innovation in aviation. I look for when the airline industry learns to fly passenger planes in the mesosphere.

They can circulate the globe with longitudinal flights between outer atmosphere and space, the time and distance covered by reducing the friction with the vacuum in space.

We must design a fleet of aircraft that can sustain reentry. These things are some of the visions given by God. All I can say is that it is truly a gift. Realize that for a long time I thought I was crazy.

I wonder about the promises of God to match us up with a perfect eternal mate, for each of us to marvel in his or her magnificent spiritual splendor. We are by far one of His most amazing creations, to face turmoil with each other, always having each other's back, to embrace each other in God's presence.

I could only imagine such a union lasting the ages. I bow before God, praying that our mistakes will not be at the risk of wounding our own descendants. If a child's roots are not deep enough by then, any swift wind will topple them.

I was that seed buried in shallow ground. The only problem was I buried myself on top of a boulder of pain. Only time, pressure, and perseverance determine how tall my tree grows. That stock engulfing the boulder deep beneath my roots has made me one sturdy rock and one unmovable tree.

Something that I prayed for was to serve in that army, to be a prince in my Heavenly Father's brigade. This dream has become reality for me, finding everything that I have written to be truth—letting my children know that you may know God intimately, that He does not leave your thoughts, that He needs you as part of a large organism of trees.

We must be the symbolism of a forest never toppled, given abundance when it is time to harvest. We shall be a sanctuary for all the birds of the sky, the squirrels of the land, so they may find shelter in this good fertile forest. This will someday become Christianity, the largest organization in the universe, and all religions will combine as one congregation on a footstool where the King, the Lord Jesus Christ awaits.

Because if you don't love, honor, and obey Him, you will serve an eternity in hell.

The United States is not going to allow civilizations to fail at critical junctures in their existence, allowing people to learn from their mistakes, while correcting a problem.

Technology is about letting human growth catch up with mechanical spirit, allowing it to grow from under our wings, making the oceans serve us.

We shall live in this world during very turbulent times. When a mechanical device could change the world if the United States had working prototypes, then miracles can happen, people will be saved. My solution to this energy problem was explained during the promotion of this manuscript.

Always respect and represent your faith in the Lord Jesus Christ, the Holy Spirit, and our Heavenly Father. Jesus Christ will be eternally with us always. My values are at the core of changing events in a new sense of direction, that our lives may have a chance to perpetuate life into different habits of thought.

Our actions can change the destination of time, the way we live in it, revealing the life worth living, the power of giving, and the answer worth receiving. Each child taken from me is a dark presence in the force of nature that connects all living things. With great knowledge comes great responsibility, so don't turn children against me.

The moment my children were taken from me; they must know how much I think of them. I loved them very much, and as their father, I was a good God-fearing foolish man. I pray that one day, God willing, I will be with them once again and they can forgive me.

That should be enough warmth to make the world snuggle at night. The forces that propel this plan will be water traveling at hundreds of feet per second, boiling at extremely high temperatures, thereby capturing kinetic energy.

Steam will billow as the reactor sends treated water from one plant, converting it into energy, multiplying, and then condensing it back to liquid, sending the process through a drag net of obstacles, hydro duct-spinning turbines that produce the heating elements to boil the water repeatedly.

This is something given to me. Visions show that inside this large vacuum, we can produce massive amounts of energy with drinkable water for children of the deserts. No pollution, only pure energy. I wait to see if this accomplishment holds true.

Heal instead of hurting, other third world countries out there they couldn't stand the temptation so, they turn their main exports from produce to illegal drugs. They feel repressed by anger, greed, and envy. I have the technology to sanitize this earth, cleansing it with clean water to drink. Thermonuclear energy can create a clean way of living.

I know all the fathers who have died in far-off beaches, jungles, oceans, and deserts, who place their hands upon the cross so that all good men and women can feel free. Jesus Christ wants all men and women to stand hand in hand, conquering the world's problems.

Whoever should believe in the Lord Jesus Christ shall not falter, yet will hold each other, standing stronger than our weakest link. Too many of them remain forever in the cold, without warmth to bind them, when we can bring heat to their homes and snow to their doorsteps.

It will be in the day when we unite under one governing body, when we centralize the United Nations in the middle of this great humanitarian effort (the United States) to supply the world with sustenance.

We must have a majority vote to approve the purifications of our river basins, the power of water currents to usable energy. Creating the process of thermonuclear coolants that propel steam, creating a beam of energy expelled beyond the core of device, geothermal, solar electric, chilled water, conditioner, a power generating apparatus.

This discussion must be implemented before Satan's representative is present and speaking, turning others against the will of God.

This dream is a thought, and these thoughts come from visions and explanations from these spirits that surround me.

If this plan sounds crude, it is because the process of humanity is such that either we think with our pride instead of our hearts, or we live in superiority of others instead of one governing body. Remember, we must be as strong as our weakest link, and this includes me. I am psychologically capable to speak to you about cold fusion.

THE END

Please spread the word if you liked the book. We are hoping for this to become a bestseller with the *New York Times*, so please tell your family and friends about this amazing manuscript. Thanks.

Shawn E. Lange

IMPORTANT PAGE WRITE REVIEW!

To e-mail the author: ShawnLange36@yahoo.com

Post a review on my website, thanks.

Website: www.ShawnLange.com

Actively seeking literary agents

Facebook account: AngelicMessengerbook https://www.facebook.com/Redfishmen

To order more books and audible music cd's: go to SHAWNLANGE.COM

Tell every person you know to purchase this manuscript.

Printed in the USA
CPSIA information can be obtained
at www.ICGtesting.com
LVHW072122280923
759462LV00001B/3